continued

Language and Literacy Series, *continued*

Literacy and History in Action

Immersive Approaches
to Disciplinary Thinking,
Grades 5–12

Thomas M. McCann
Rebecca D'Angelo
Nancy Galas
Mary Greska

Foreword by Peter Smagorinsky

TEACHERS COLLEGE PRESS

TEACHERS COLLEGE | COLUMBIA UNIVERSITY
NEW YORK AND LONDON

Published by Teachers College Press, 1234 Amsterdam Avenue, New York, NY 10027

Copyright © 2015 by Teachers College, Columbia University

Library of Congress Cataloging-in-Publication Data

McCann, Thomas M., author.
    Literacy and history in action : immersive approaches to disciplinary thinking,
        grades 5–12 / Thomas M. McCann, Rebecca D'Angelo, Nancy Galas, & Mary
        Greska.
            pages cm. — (Language and literacy series)
    Includes bibliographical references and index.
    ISBN 978-0-8077-5734-5 (pbk. : alk. paper)
    ISBN 978-0-8077-5735-2 (hardcover : alk. paper)
    ISBN 978-0-8077-7431-1 (ebook)
        1. History—Study and teaching (Elementary)—United States. 2. History—
    Study and teaching (Secondary)—United States. 3. Literacy—Study and
    teaching—United States. 4. Language arts—Correlation with content subjects.
    I. Title.
    LB1582.U6M57   2015
    372.89—dc23   2015023366

ISBN 978-0-8077-5734-5 (paper)
ISBN 978-0-8077-5735-2 (hardcover)
ISBN 978-0-8077-7431-1 (ebook)

Printed on acid-free paper
Manufactured in the United States of America

22   21   20   19   18   17   16   15   8   7   6   5   4   3   2   1

Contents

Foreword

At one point during my years as a high school English teacher, I became enamored of the idea of Writing Across the Curriculum. As a writer, I had experienced the psychic rush of having my unfolding prose generate ideas that had not yet coalesced in my thinking, but emerged through the process of articulating them. Wouldn't it be great, I thought, if teachers across the curriculum included writing in their students' work so that the whole range of disciplines could produce such insights and discoveries in students' engagement with schoolwork?

I realized when talking to teachers in other disciplines, however, that the last thing they wanted was another imposition forced on them by outsiders who did not understand their domain. Science teachers, for instance, talked about how their discipline often relied on diagrams that demonstrated the flow of elements in a physical space. This illustration shows how a science teacher, for instance, might help students learn about the digestive system.

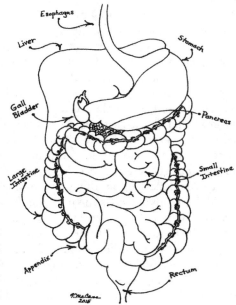

Science teachers would become downright peeved when told that kids would learn more by writing across the curriculum. They believed that students might learn *less* if forced to undertake the laborious process of writing to explain what they could easily depict in a diagram. Further, science teachers would be put in the position of becoming graders of grammar, mechanics, and usage—a task for which they often felt unprepared.

It began to dawn on me at such times that perhaps writing has a disciplinary dimension that we were all overlooking—that writing conventions varied along with the other demands of thinking in the disciplines, and that what counts as good writing for an English teacher might be quite different from what counts as good writing for people in Science and History. This idea of the disciplinary demands made on writers was being developed by others at the time (e.g., Bazerman & Paradis, 1991), although not in ways that reached many high school faculties. Although the concept that writing in History and writing in Science follow different rules and customs has since gotten wider acceptance, persuading teachers across the curriculum to think of themselves as writing teachers has remained a hard sell.

Perhaps, though, there are ways to think about writing so that it's less oriented to a discipline's historical genre expectations and more oriented to problem-solving as a way of thinking. Enter Tom, Becky, Nancy, and Mary and this impressive approach to thinking about history as a problem-solving subject. They conceive of history as a dynamic subject, rather than as a fact-oriented discipline. Historical events are open to interpretation and require the ability to see the world from multiple perspectives in order to be understood in a well-rounded, well-informed fashion. Role-playing games are ideally suited for this task, and include a variety of benefits as well. This book, centered on three compelling scenarios that provide the roles and dilemmas for the activities, both provides teachers with material that they can adapt to their classes as written, and also models a process for writing new activities that allow for the exploration of other conflicts arising in historical settings.

Constructing a strong role-playing game, say the authors, is available to anyone with knowledge of the world and an active imagination. First, a setting for the event should be established, and for historical purposes, this environment should map onto the known reality of the focal circumstances as closely as possible. The activity then requires characters to populate the setting, perhaps real and perhaps fabricated; historical knowledge should help winnow out anachronistic elements and make the situation as authentic as possible, so that, for instance, colonial rebels do not contact one another via cellphone. The next task is to determine the fundamental challenge facing the characters in this setting, and to then elaborate on how the problem gets increasingly complex as it becomes filtered through a variety of perspectives as relevant information gets introduced. This challenge is thus channeled through a given social process, such as the introduction of a bill, a meeting of a town council, or another civic confluence of people, place, and problem.

This forum provides the medium through which students engage in discussion and may be face-to-face or virtual. These discussions involve writing for the purpose of generating and contrasting ideas during the initial process of thinking through the issues, and also provide the initial drafts that may be developed into more formal writing. This writing might be exploratory in the initial stages, and then take a position to argue as the issues become increasingly clear. Ultimately, additional writing may prompt students to reflect on their learning, the justness of the process, their developing under-standings of the issues, and other pertinent matters.

The authors then provide three illustrations of how this process has generated for them a set of role-playing simulations—using the topics of European engagement and conflict with the Native people of North America, the dilemma faced by pre-Revolution colonists, and the challenges of the Civil War and Reconstruction. The scenarios involve deliberations about going to war to settle intractable conflicts between European incursionists to North America and three sets of antagonists.

The authors present this volume as a way to teach history and how to engage with and evaluate it, but its application is potentially much broader. I propose some extensions that could work across the curriculum so that writing is an organic part of disciplinary life, rather than an add-on that takes teachers out of their element.

Science. Science is a field in flux that includes an essayist tradition taken up by Stephen Jay Gould, Lewis Thomas, and others that goes beyond the reporting of experiments or observations and considers such matters as the morality in scientific inquiry. Global warming, water restrictions, industry regulations on pollution, and many other topics have the potential for devel-opment into scenarios in which the issues are debated and student writing may emerge.

English. Tom McCann has been using scenario-based activities for English classes as a way to provide students with ways of thinking about problems that arise in their engagement with literary themes. These scenarios are typ-ically complex and often involve moral reasoning. Students may discuss, for example, a family dilemma in which a pet has reached a point of decline that must be resolved, possibly through euthanasia, and the implications of this decision for all family members. His work is abundantly available to provide additional models for teachers to draw on to help students think their way through the real-life issues raised in their responses to literature and other texts.

Art. Art is often controversial. As I write this Foreword, the nation is still affected by an art contest in which first prize went to the best cartoon of the prophet Mohammed, a depiction not allowed or tolerated in Islam. I can imagine a scenario that would divide students into a set of compet-ing perspectives on the contest: the meeting in which sponsors discuss their planning of the event, a meeting involving a group of Muslims who find the event offensive and sacrilegious, a discussion among law officers called in to patrol the event, a gathering of journalists sent to cover the event, a meeting of the competition's judges, or another set of stakeholders. Many other artistic works could similarly form the basis for role-playing activities.

Mathematics. Mathematics figures into important civic decisions, such as taxation rates, budgets, measurements, calculations, fees, and countless (ho-ho) other ways of reaching decisions based on crunching numbers. The school budget, for instance, or more manageably the students' class budget, could be the subject of discussion and argumentation, as could the cost of running concessions at school-sponsored events and other cost-benefit analyses.

Home Economics. Students could hold forums on the question of food additives (GMO ingredients, preservatives, dyes, etc.), organic vs. synthetic or chemically produced foods, the role of meat in diet, the economics of growing meat vs. plants for food, the ingredients in school breakfasts, and countless other issues related to the domestic budget and operation of the home.

Foreign Language. The United States currently provides a cauldron of possibilities for discussing the role of non-English languages in U.S. society, from street signs in Chinatown, to signage in international airports, to instructions on products, to bilingual education, to English-Only rules.

This terrific book helps teachers think about how to design instruction to provide an education across the curriculum that is provocative and stimulating, and that helps young people develop both the thinking and writing skills they will need to succeed in their persuasion. I love this book, and wish I were still in the classroom to use both its examples and its principles in my own planning. I look forward to hearing how its readers use and adapt these lessons in their teaching, and how their students engage with and make sense of the possibilities these activities afford.

—Peter Smagorinsky

Acknowledgments

During the time that we were drafting this book, Tom's old friend and mentor George Hillocks Jr. passed away. We appreciate George's considerable and consistent guidance over many years, and we are especially grateful for his affirmation and encouragement with the current project. He was particularly positive about lessons that can actively involve learners in processes of discovery and that prepared these young people for producing some remarkable writing. In writing about inductive or discovery learning long ago, George observed that one important value in a discovery approach is that students experienced *excitement* about their learning, and he insisted that this sense of exhilaration during learning was every student's *right*. We hope that this book serves as a testament to George's lasting influence on teachers and learners, and we trust that the instructional practices that we showcase are consistent with the learner-centered principles that he long espoused.

We are also grateful to Marjorie Hillocks, who visited our school as a drama teacher consultant. We judge that the drama activities in which Marjie involved our students helped them to empathize with characters, assume temporary identities, and live the experience imagined in a simulated environment. In many ways, Marjie helped us to transport our students into significant moments in our nation's history.

During the development of the simulations and the writing of individual chapters, Dr. Alan C. Jones generously read what we had written and offered insightful advice. As a former middle school and high school social studies teacher and keen judge about what appeals to learners and fosters their inquiries and discoveries, Al provided reliable suggestions, cautions, and encouragement. We have also leaned on our friends Elizabeth Kahn and Joe Flanagan for their useful judgments about the individual lessons and sequences that would help students to learn discipline-specific content as they developed mature literacy practices. We value their steady friendship and reliable professional judgments.

We are indebted to Peter Smagorinsky for his generous Foreword and his insights and encouragement as we developed the book. We appreciate Peter's affirmation of the ideas promoted in this book, and we cherish his enduring friendship.

Mary, Nancy, and Becky thank Dr. Bhavna Sharma-Lewis for bringing them together as an instructional team and for encouraging years of professional collaboration. We are also grateful to our friends and colleagues Laura Ryan and Lisa Mariani, who have bravely taken these journeys into history with us and patiently countenanced our complicating their already complicated lives as teachers. We also thank Jim Pluskota for his support of our professional endeavors.

Tom has depended on the insights of his university colleagues John Knapp, Judy Pokorny, Brad Peters, Laura Bird, and Amy Levin, during almost daily conversations about teaching and engaging the minds of young learners. Tom is grateful to these colleagues for their reliable advice, positive outlooks, and steady encouragement.

We are indebted to Teachers College Press editor Emily Spangler for her steady guidance and support through the long process of completing this project. We are also grateful for the assistance of Karl Nyberg, Noelle de la Paz, Emily Renwick, Nancy Power, Michael McGann, and others on the editorial, marketing, and production staffs of Teachers College Press.

The patience, support, and indulgence of our families have encouraged us to see this project through to completion. We are especially grateful to our constant cheerleader Pam McCann, who lives in the moment and lets others fuss about the details.

Literacy and History in Action

Learning in Action

Three classes assembled together in the school's library to enact a simulated legislative hearing about a proposed bill that would provide reparations for Native Americans. Teams of students had researched specific tribes and were set to offer testimony about the qualities of each tribe's culture and to report the harms that the tribe had suffered at the hands of non-Native settlers to North America and from an apparently unsympathetic U.S. government. A team of students representing "experts" offered testimony about the Sioux Nation. One student concluded the presentation:

> *Evan:* We think the Sioux would feel better with a sincere apology. We think the reservations should be nicer for the Sioux so the Sioux need funding for better houses. If they can get the Black Hills back, this would be the best reparation because that land has always been sacred to the Sioux. Also, scholarships for the Sioux for college or training and job opportunities to help break the poverty that has been passed down from generation to generation.
>
> Twenty years ago, in 1994, a white buffalo named Miracle was born on a Sioux reservation. The Sioux thought this was a sign that life of the Sioux would soon improve. We hope the legislation we encourage you to adopt can help provide the miracle for our people.
>
> *"Legislator 1":* If we return land to the Sioux tribe, what will become of the people who now live on that land?
>
> *Evan:* They will just have to move, the way that the Sioux were forced to move long ago. The government can compensate people for the homes they have to leave.
>
> *Nicole:* In a lot of places in the Black Hills there is no one living there, because it is not places that you would want to farm. So you would just be buying the homes from a few people.
>
> *Niko:* White people moved there a long time ago and took the land from the Sioux because they thought that there was gold. Since there isn't any gold there today, people have moved away.

The testimonies and the question-and-answer exchanges continued until the participants had heard about six tribes and the experience of non-Native settlers in North America. In the following chapters, we report on this simulation and similar learning activities to reveal how students' active participation in "living" the experience of history prompted their extensive research, critical reading, and elaborated writing. We have developed and refined a series of simulations that engage students in inquiry and purpose-driven reading, writing, and speaking. We describe both the activity structures and the students in action as they imagined what Native Americans have experienced, what pre–Revolutionary War colonists endured, and what Americans who lived during the Civil War and Reconstruction must have witnessed.

Our experience together years ago in a professional development workshop on the teaching of writing led to an enduring teaching partnership. Inspired by the workshop, we knew we wanted to expand writing instruction with our students. The perennial problem was how to add instruction to a curriculum that was already packed. Our solution was to integrate writing into social studies. While we expected to benefit from the natural efficiencies of doing so, we were pleasantly surprised by the extent and quality of the writing that students produced (see examples in the coming chapters), and we were struck by mutually beneficial curriculum overlap between literacy learning and content learning. We also concluded that we must be providing students in 5th grade with a rich and enduring learning experience when many of them returned to visit us after they had advanced to middle school and reported their impression that "the kids from our school knew so much more than kids from other schools" when it came to understanding the events that led to the Revolutionary War. Year after year, we saw evidence that students were developing as writers and were learning much about U.S. history. But we saw much more. Students were reading several related texts, recalling and evaluating what they read, expressing themselves lucidly in conversation, listening carefully to other speakers, and generally participating in civil and rational ways in the daily discourse of the classroom. These advanced literacy experiences, all of which align with the Common Core State Standards, even for high school, prepared students for their own elaborated writing. We noticed too that students were talking in a mature way about issues, such as distinguishing schools of political thought and judging competing political, economic, and ethical values, that one would normally think of as topics for adult conversation, all in a process consistent with the democratic procedures that Parker (2003) describes and aligned with the C3 Framework for social studies standards for civic literacy. And students seemed to be enjoying themselves in a process that seemed more like play than schoolwork. In this book we share how our students and we teachers came to this state of active and engaged learning.

At its core, this book shares three extended simulation activities that immerse students in three eras of U.S. history: European incursions into North America, pre-Revolution colonialism, and the Civil War and Reconstruction. We are not historians. Our interest has been to help students to think critically and communicate in complex ways as they learn significant content. In the study of elements of U.S. history, we wanted students to develop mature practices as readers and writers. Of course, writers operate with purpose, write about some substance, and address specific audiences in a specified context. As teachers of writing, we knew that offering generic strategies or exemplary models of writing would have little effect on the writing of our students unless they knew something of substance to write about: to be able to frame problems and recognize competing views, to cite data of various sorts to support generalizations, to interpret data, and to select language appropriate for a given audience. These proficiencies are consistent with the skills suggested by the Common Core Standards for reading and writing; they are also procedures that are part of civic literacy, enabling participants to measure fairly the competing perspectives on an issue and collaborate in problem solving. As we planned to infuse writing instruction into social studies content, we learned much about history ourselves and saw that students were more engaged than ever with the social studies concepts and historical content. But our intent here is not to transmit a social studies curriculum ready-made for a specific grade level. While some teachers might be able to adapt the activities for their own classrooms, we don't expect that anyone will adopt the materials wholesale as part of a social studies or literacy curriculum. Instead, we hope to show the promise of simulations as powerful tools for literacy and content learning, and to reveal a model for such instructional experiences so that teachers can adapt the approach for the specific content and literacy goals within their own schools. The examples of discussion-based inquiry activities might guide teachers in their design of units that emphasize different content (e.g., the suffrage movement, Prohibition and the rise of organized crime, the Cold War, the War in Vietnam, or the aftermath of 9/11). We expect that this book will reveal possibilities for instructional activities that immerse students in content study requiring action and interaction.

THE POWER OF SIMULATIONS

Simulations are not new. They have been used as promising instructional tools in teaching learners how to do potentially dangerous things (e.g., driving a car, flying a plane) in a protected simulated environment. In more conventional classrooms, teachers have relied on simulations to imitate environments and situations for learning everything from medical procedures to business management strategies. The work of Lynn Quitman Troyka especially interested us. In a 1974 study, Troyka reports that students in composition classes in a community college experienced impressive growth as academic writers when they participated in a series of simulation role-playing activities during the course of a semester of study. Later Troyka and Nudelman shared a series of such activities in a book called *Taking Action* (1975), which supported teachers' efforts to advance students' speaking, listening, reading, and writing skills.

Hillocks discusses Troyka's study in his *Research on Written Composition* (1986), categorizing the instructional approach as *inquiry*. As participants in inquiry, the students in the Troyka study learned specific procedures (e.g., comparative advantage analysis, comparison/contrast, argument, classification) as they tackled "real-world" problems together, responding to issues of governance, economics, and social responsibility. These problems included a government's budget crisis, the environmental impact of a chemical company operating near a resort area, an uprising in a prison facility, and the staffing of a police force. The students had abundant information to support their effort and wrote for a specific audience in order to advance a specific goal. In planning our instruction, we looked to Troyka's examples, and we checked our planned simulations against Gee's (2007) descriptions of the design grammar that directs the engineering of highly engrossing video games. Essentially, we wanted students to be aware of a tangible and ultimately attainable goal. We wanted to equip students with the tools that they needed to accomplish their goal, and we expected that learners would be able to assess regularly the status of their progress toward that goal. Above all, we expected that students would talk to one another a great deal, and through this purposeful talk they would figure out where they stand in regard to great historical and contemporary perplexities (e.g., deciding reparations, responding to oppression, reconstructing a torn nation) and would practice the procedures for evaluating the arguments of other people and advancing their own arguments with relevant evidence and appropriate interpretations. These procedures for evaluating the written and spoken arguments of others and advancing one's own arguments hold a special place in the Common Core State Standards and are key to the disciplinary thinking in history and politics.

In one form or another, simulations have been common in social studies classrooms for years (e.g., Charles & Stadsklev, 1973; Garvey & Garvey, 1967; Shaffer, Squire, Halverson, & Gee, 2005). We judge that the kind of discussion- and inquiry-based learning activities illustrated in this book share similarities with the kind of history learning and teaching that Wineburg, Martin, and Monte-Sano (2013) recommend. We also suggest that students' active participation in the kind of learning experiences that immerse students in extensive and varied dialogue of the kind that we illustrate throughout the book are consistent with Walter Parker's notion of "teaching democracy" (2003, 2010). Parker notes that deliberation is a creative act that allows students to experience democratic processes and spirit:

It is an occasion—an experience—that happens between persons. It is not defined solely by its substantive aim, which is to choose wisely and fairly a course of action, nor solely by the deliberative methods employed, but also by the way it constitutes a relationship—a purposeful relationship that requires some measure of getting to know one another, presenting ourselves to one another, expressing opinions and reasons for them, and listening, whether we are particularly fond of one another or not. Consequently, deliberation is not a means to an end (reaching a decision), but an end in itself, for it creates a particular kind of democratic public culture among the deliberators. (2003, p. 80)

This is the kind of classroom environment we have tried to foster—a place where students can together grapple with tough issues, sometimes disagreeing, but in a civil and rational way, learning complex ways of communicating and productive and constructive means of problem solving.

The discussion-based simulations that we share in this book, in a sense, involve students in play, but this play is not to be confused with frivolity or activity for activity's sake. Vygotsky (1978) notes that "in play a child always acts above his average age, above his daily behavior; in play it is as though he were a head taller than himself" (p. 102). Vygotsky's comments apply both to very young children and to adolescents (p. 104). For Holzman (2009) and Elkind (2007), play has the power both to stretch learners above their daily behavior and to foster confidence that they can enter, at least temporarily, into adult roles. The kind of play that the simulations offer helps students to grow academically as well as socially and emotionally. If we think of play as something other than forms of amusement that give one pleasure, we can see play in structures that require conforming to rules and functioning in a role beyond everyday practice, as in a variety of games, including those that can ultimately disappoint us. The simulations project school-age learners into various adult roles (e.g., experts testifying before a committee, family members making decisions and reporting them in town hall deliberations, travelers finding their way home across a war-torn landscape). The activities propel students into roles beyond their current identity, with the support of their peers and their teachers. When students accept the conditions of the simulated environment, they also readily try out their roles within this environment—as historical expert, as colonist, as Civil War survivor—and act as they imagine one should act in these adult roles.

We judge also that the simulations as examples of learning activities conform to what Newmann, Marks, and Gamoran (1996) call "authentic pedagogy." In the process of assuming a role, tackling problems, researching positions, and judging the contributions of others, students learn much about history, writing, speaking, listening, and reading. They construct their understandings and learn procedures that apply to tasks in other classes and in their daily lives. They engage with their classmates in disciplined inquiry, both through their collaborations with classmates and through their individual efforts.

The use of simulations involves students in extensive classroom talk. We understand from the work of Nystrand (1997), Juzwik, Borsheim-Black, Caughlan, and Heintz (2013), Langer (2001), Applebee and Langer (2013), and McCann (2014) that extensive purposeful talk—authentic discussion—in classrooms and through online extensions helps students to advance their literacy skills and prepares them to perform well on assessments of reading and writing. The simulations structure the occasions for authentic discussion by setting purpose, supporting efforts, encouraging participation, fostering the interchange of diverse views, and leading to synthesis and reflection.

In reflecting on any of our attempts to cultivate rich discussions in our classrooms, we recall that there have always been the more active players and the more diffident observers. While we want to promote environments for active learning, we recognize that active engagement in learning does not have to mean that all students are talking a lot or otherwise contributing in some overt way. We recognize from the work of Schultz (2009) that students can "participate" in a variety of ways. For example, during a simulated town hall meeting, students on the outside of the circle of deliberators can pass notes to their representatives. During the simulated legislative hearings, some students not presenting to the panel post comments on a blog. When it comes to participating in current social and political debates while remaining outside the panel of discussants, we can draw from our own experience. As listeners to NPR's *Diane Rhem Show*, we can attest to our captivated participation in the exchanges between on-air panelists, even when we don't call into the show. We benefit from hearing the exchange of ideas, perhaps beginning with our presumptions and prejudices before informed experts contribute information and analysis, adjusting and refining our perspectives as we hear nuanced arguments, challenges, and defenses. Similarly, when we listen to Nina Totenberg report on a session of the U.S. Supreme Court, we find ourselves participants as we listen to contending litigants and probing justices and try to sort out for ourselves the balance between national security interests and the necessary protections of privacy rights, and other such debates. But this type of quiet participation is possible only when thoughtful dialogue is present to witness.

FEATURES OF STRONG SIMULATIONS

We understand from looking at a variety of simulations and from working with our own examples that a well-designed simulation activity that promotes dialogue will have a few key features. We list those features here and highlight them throughout the following chapters.

- *Construct a Specific Environment:* Students enter into an imagined environment that has its own characteristics, rules, and constraints. For example, living in an 18th-century Colonial town will define how one communicates, travels, and calculates the value of currency. At a legislative hearing, students follow some formalities and use selected language to adapt to a particular audience and forum.
- *Form Identities:* Part of the pedagogical value of the simulation is that it forces students to pay attention to different points of view, introducing complexity and promoting critical thinking. While teachers outline the parameters of the identities of the players, students typically enjoy fleshing out the details of their individual and family identities. Students recognize identity formation as a common element in video games, and they readily accept that the identity for the game is distinct from their own identity and, in many cases, even relish the distinctive characteristics.
- *Frame Problems:* The simulation introduces a broad problem (survival, completing a journey, passing a bill) that involves several subsidiary problems, which include management tasks, communication responsibilities, and even ethical dilemmas.
- *Provide Information:* Students tackle problems with the support of relevant information, which a teacher can supply or the students find as a stage in the process.
- *Structure a Pathway:* The broad structure of the simulation suggests a trajectory (e.g., the process of moving a bill through a legislative process, a journey home or to a new community, the inescapable movement toward war). Students will recognize such structures from games, including video games that are popular with some students.
- *Design Forums:* The central dynamic of the simulation is the dialogue among peers. Students engage in team problem solving and group deliberation. These opportunities for discussion can include online environments in which students post blogs, participate in discussion forums, and collaborate in wiki spaces. The discussions involve students in processes that transfer to writing and to reading: defining abstract concepts, evaluating the behavior of characters and groups, judging the most efficacious policy, and weighing the relative merits of options, among others.
- *Provide for Synthesis and Reflection:* At the end of a process, participants have opportunities to reflect on what happened and how they were able to accomplish what they did. A writing prompt might ask the learners to draw from an extended experience to judge its meaning; another writing prompt or discussion might ask students how they solved problems, found information, judged values, and produced elaborated compositions.

In accounting for the powerful effect the simulations in the Troyka study had on student writing, Hillocks observes, "The structure of the learning environment established by the teacher and the materials simplifies the task of developing an appropriate argument by taking over some part of the task" (1993, p. 256). The teacher simplifies matters by introducing problems and directing students to the information that they need in order to tackle the problems together. But it is the dynamic of peer interaction that helps students to command important literacy procedures and inquiry processes essential to history study. Hillocks further observes, "As they present arguments to one another, students will see how those coming at the same issue from a different perspective will respond to their arguments. In the process, they learn more about developing a complete argument" (p. 256). Consistent with Hillocks, Graham and Perin (2007) and Applebee and Langer (2013) note that students learn important procedures for writing as they collaborate with one another in a supportive environment. We believe that we have created situations for the collision of competing views, but we also hope that we have constructed forums and protocols for sorting out conflicts through civil and rational means.

We are encouraged that the Common Core State Standards emphasize rigorous reading, writing, listening, and speaking goals. We know that the simulations that we have followed with our students have engaged them in demanding tasks involving the reading of complex texts (both fiction and informational, including primary source documents), deliberating in rich speaking and listening exchanges among peers, thinking critically, and writing extensively. We also appreciate that the C3 Framework (National Council for Social Studies [NCSS], 2013) summarizes a set of integrated concepts and procedures that move the conception of social studies beyond the recall of bodies of information, and we judge that students learn those concepts and procedures when they are involved in purposeful inquiry with their peers. Inquiry is at the heart of the C3 Framework: "CENTRAL to a rich social studies experience is the capability for developing questions that CAN FRAME AND ADVANCE AN INQUIRY. Those questions come in two forms: compelling and supporting questions" (p. 24, emphasis in original). The simulations offered in this book show all students, whether labeled "gifted" or "regular," as being active in shared investigations into several questions that the learners find engaging and that have significance within their community. Students attend to competing perspectives, consult and evaluate several sources of information, and form reasoned judgments. They develop procedures for telling the story of events and assessing the significance and effect of those events. They learn how systems of government work and how these systems can serve as engines of social change. Their grappling with the problems introduced by the teacher in turn influences students to generate their own questions about what has happened in the past, why conditions are the way they are at the moment, and how they can join with others in making matters better.

FEATURES OF WRITING INSTRUCTION

In designing content-rich and discussion-based simulations intended to prepare learners for writing extensive compositions, we have tried to honor
what we understand to be key elements of effective writing instruction. We
judge that the instructional activities that we share here align with principles
of a *structured process* approach to writing instruction (Applebee, 1986;
Smagorinsky, Johannessen, Kahn, & McCann, 2010). Applebee (1986)
associates a structured process approach with Hillocks (1984, 1986) and
contrasts this approach with a more generic process of planning, drafting,
revising, editing, and publishing, or with what Hillocks calls a "natural process" stance. A structured process approach to writing instruction would be
specific to the procedures that are necessary for producing a specific kind
of text for a specific audience. The process would attend to the kind of
knowledge the writer needs in order to produce a particular kind of text in
a particular context. In attempting to stay true to a structured process, we
have emphasized the following instructional features:

- *Emphasis on teaching procedures that are generative:* Instead of
  emphasizing models and generic forms for writing, we engage
  students in problem solving so they can develop and practice
  the appropriate procedures for the given situation: narrating,
  explaining, arguing, evaluating, and so on.
- *Purposeful and frequent peer interaction:* Learners develop procedures
  for composing through the regular dialogue with peers. The talk
  among peers exposes students to various points of view, enriches
  the conversation with multiple sources of information, and allows
  for the oral rehearsal of processes that transfer into writing.
- *Inquiry and critical thinking:* The entire simulation process is
  essentially inquiry, in that there is a problem or area of doubt at the
  center of a purposeful investigation and productive deliberation.
  The investigation into the problem (e.g., defining and judging
  reparations, determining policy, evaluating ethical action) drives the
  action of the simulation and guides the procedures that transform
  into written expression.
- *Narrative representation of problems:* Problems take compelling form
  when they come alive in a specific context, with real characters and
  recognizable conflicts. The richness of the imagined world of the
  simulation transports students as players into real human dramas.
- *Scaffolded instructional activities and discussions:* As students engage
  in discussions and learn related procedures, they build on these
  procedures to move on to new challenges and levels of complexities.
  Each discussion has a purpose, which has to be served in order for
  students to move on to a new stage in the dialogic process (e.g.,

defining the concept of *reparations* before applying this standard in proposing the policy for responding to offending characters or communities).

- ***Process-orientated follow-through:*** While the extensive talk among students is critical in their learning procedures and practicing their expression of judgments and reporting of events, a composing process extends from this talk and includes individual planning, drafting, sharing with peers and teachers, and refining efforts. The process might include a formal "publication" or other means of showcasing what students have written.

In describing processes in the following chapters, we highlight these features as specific to writing instruction, but also consistent with inquiry into social studies. We recognize and intend that the practices we describe blur the line between literacy instruction and content instruction, but we want to identify certain elements as particularly important supports for students' development as writers. We see that the written responses to the complex historical issues support our efforts to assess students' learning and serve as learners' tools for forming judgments and synthesizing what they have learned.

PURPOSE-DRIVEN LITERACY

The examples in this book show 5th-graders at work, but our experience with students from 5th grade through college is that they learn the complexities of making inferences, critically evaluating what they read, and writing meaningful elaborated compositions because they have a *purpose* for doing so. We wonder whether attempts to teach students abstract strategies for reading (e.g., envisioning, questioning, predicting, comparing) and generic models for writing can succeed when students have no genuine purpose for attempting these imposed literacy efforts.

Robert Shepherd warns against the trivialization of complicated literacy processes: "No kid walks away from his or her Making Inferences lesson with any substantive learning, with any world knowledge or concept or set of procedures that can actually be applied in order to determine what kind of inference a particular one is and whether that inference is reasonable" (Ravitch, 2013). In other words, inferencing is often complex and not suitable to generic formulas. Similarly, Hillocks warns that the emphasis on exposing students to abstract forms of writing—usually through models, templates, or abstract rubrics—fails to imbue the composing effort with purpose. He reminds us, "The problem, of course, is that writers do not decide to write an expository paragraph or an evaluative theme. If they decide to write prose at all, they decide to write about specific subject matter.

Moreover, knowledge of form does not translate into the strategies and skills necessary to wrest from the subject matter the ideas that make up a piece of writing" (2005, p. 238).

Dewey (1998) long ago noted the importance of giving learners a sense of the purpose for their learning. Purpose helps to define the quality of experience and the interactions with peers. Referring to living in an experience, Dewey observes:

> It means, once more, that interaction is going on between an individual and objects and other persons. The conceptions of situation and of interaction are inseparable from each other. An experience is always what it is because of a transaction taking place between an individual and what, at the time, constitutes his environment, whether the latter consists of persons with whom he is talking about some topic or event, the subject talked about being also a part of the situation. (p. 41)

Dewey (2008) also notes that if students are going to experience the "associated life" that distinguishes a democracy, they will need to experience democratic processes, seeing how decisions can be negotiated and feeling how the decisions of an individual or a group necessarily affect the lives of others connected through the democratic web of mutuality.

We judge that students' experiences in the playful learning that simulations offer provide students with a clear purpose for talking at length with others, even their perceived debate opponents; tackling complex texts; and writing elaborated compositions. We have also seen that the involvement in simulation activities of the sort that we offer here will support teachers in their efforts to promote social and emotional goals, especially those that emphasize the skills of positive social interactions, respectful attention to diverse perspectives, and advocacy for the general good of the community. In essence, we see the students' learning through their involvement in simulations as an intersection between affect and cognition. We have seen students time and again extend their classroom experience by tackling some unsolicited project of their own choosing, and they are consistently eager to set aside other school and classroom routines to enter a simulated world where others appreciate what they know, allow them some choice, and connect them to a community seeking shared goals.

THINKING BIG

In designing curricula for schools, many teachers and curriculum coordinators may have been influenced by Wiggins and McTighe (2005, 2013) and Burke (2010), who urge teachers to attend with their students to the "essential questions" or "big ideas" that distinguish the lines of inquiry in particular disciplines. The activities in the following chapters help students to explore some overarching questions that we understand to be important not only to historians who look into the past but also to contemporary thinkers who are debating current questions and deliberating about policy decisions. We expect that students will give all sides of a question a fair hearing, accurately represent several views in summary form, evaluate competing policy positions and interpretations of events, and explain to others how they have arrived at their conclusions. We judge that for both teachers and students, keeping big questions and priority standards in mind will be far more useful than trying to make an inventory of all the individual skills and bits of information, which will naturally be subsumed under the broad inquiry effort. We have not relied on daily paper-and-pencil tests to check that students have recalled or connected some details about events. In our assessments, we have focused primarily on evidence that students have command of important procedures—arguing, summarizing, connecting, evaluating, and narrating—both in oral and written expression. We listened to discussions and presentations and examined informal and formal writing at different stages to seek evidence of procedural proficiencies. In order to argue, summarize, connect, evaluate, and narrate, students have to command a wealth of content knowledge, so we look for an accurate representation of events in history and an assessment of their significance.

Again, we are not offering a social studies or language arts curriculum here but are sharing some models of highly interactive classroom experiences that integrate literacy learning and content learning. In the chapters that follow, we lay out in detail some sample activities that teachers can use as models in designing similar activities that explore other issues and investigate other content. The models may also serve the purpose of stimulating discussion in which parallels are drawn between past historical issues and events and contemporary issues and events. The examples show how to frame problems that have a reasonable potential for engaging all learners, how to assemble the relevant data (including primary source texts) or build in a research stage to access information to support inquiry, and how to organize and manage discussion forums to allow students to explore compelling issues together. We expect also that the sample sequences demonstrate the power of scaffolding to help students to build on what they know and expand their thinking to make complex judgments and to communicate about their decisions in elaborated and logical ways. Table I.1 distills the activities and issues that you will encounter in the coming chapters.

FOUNDATIONAL SCAFFOLDS TO COMPLEX PROBLEMS

We hope that we have generated some interest and enthusiasm in our readers for looking into the samples of complex learning activities in this book.

Table I.1. Summary of Chapters and Simulations

Chapters	Simulation	Critical Questions	Contemporary Issues
1 and 2	Legislative Hearing: Proposed Bill for Reparations for Native Americans	How does an individual or a society repair the damages inflicted on others? When are reparations necessary? How does one determine the extent and form of reparations?	Who can be held to account for the harms perpetrated in the distant past? Must those who enjoy current privileges satisfy a debt to those who suffered harms in order to ensure those privileges?
3 and 4	Colonial Elmtown	What moved colonists to wage war with England and declare independence? How could the leaders of rebellion adequately justify their acts of defiance of authority?	When might anyone be justified in defying authority or breaking the law? What key issues separate political parties? What rights must be guaranteed to all?
5 and 6	The Road from Appomattox	What is the cost of war? What causes societies to enter into horrific wars? In a just society, how should the victors treat the vanquished?	What are the relative merits of revenge or mercy? How can a nation divided by war recover and heal wounds? What is the proper balance between states' rights and national interests?

We also want to help teachers to prepare all students for success with the tasks that each simulation requires. For example, the next chapter describes students grappling with the concept of *reparations*—attempting to express criteria for determining when reparations are necessary and what form the repair should take. The students' job in the end is to write arguments by applying their criteria to the information that they have gathered in order to draw conclusions and advance a proposition. The other simulations present similar tasks for which students have to be ready. Hillocks (2010, 2011) reminds us that the students' work (or play) in these simulations would involve both arguments of judgment (epideictic) and arguments of policy (deliberative) as students determine a particular value and use expressed criteria for guiding policy. This undertaking assumes that students have worked with at least the rudiments of argument. Obviously teachers will have to devote some time to helping students to conceive of argument as logical thinking, as opposed to verbal combat, and will need to engage students in the practice of contending with controversy in a way that is both civil and rational. We offer some suggestions below to help in accomplishing these ends.

We have found that before tackling the more complicated simulations, it is useful to practice with similar inquiry-based activities that help students to learn the procedures for argument and deliberation in simpler, more familiar backdrops. We have found the following works to be especially useful sources of problem-based activities that students enjoy and that help them to learn the procedures for argument: Hillocks's *Teaching Argument Writing, Grades 6–12* (2011); Smagorinsky, Johannessen, Kahn, and McCann's *The Dynamics of Writing Instruction* (2010) and *Teaching Students to Write Argument* (2011); and Smith, Wilhelm, and Fredricksen's *Oh, Yeah?! Putting Argument to Work Both in School and Out* (2012).

PREPARING FOR SUCCESS

Reflective teachers who are interested in following similar sequences and using the sample activities will want to plan for the measure of the effects—in the development of students' writing, in their understanding of complex texts, in their command of history concepts, in their reasoning and civility in deliberating with peers, and in the general quality of learners' experiences in the classroom. We offer sample rubrics in the online appendixes to help toward this end. All appendixes are available for free viewing and download on this book's webpage or the free downloads page at tcpress. com. We understand that any teacher will want to reflect on the effect of instruction and will want to be able to show others, especially skeptics within a school district or a community, how students advanced their speaking, listening, reading, and writing proficiencies while they engaged in learning experiences that often seem like a game and feel like play. In addition, the rubrics can serve as the basis for teachers and peers to offer feedback to students about their work in groups, their participation in the forums, and their attempts at the related writing.

We recognize that one size of curriculum does not fit all learners. We understand that all teaching and learning are bound by specific contexts (e.g., the characteristics of specific groups of learning, the constraints of a school district's policies, the physical setting, the resources of a community). While we believe that the instructional activities that we share in this book have been both fun and enriching for our students, we understand that in other school settings, the materials may have to be adapted in some ways and that student discourse might sound different from what we have experienced with our students. We think that we have followed very promising principled practices, but we don't offer a "best practice" script. Our old friend Peter Smagorinsky makes this distinction:

> When instruction is tied to principled, reflective practice, "anything goes" becomes untenable: Things only "go" if they work according to the teacher's thoughtful standard of learning or other desired result. Best practices then are comprised of the methods that a teacher determines, through principled reflection on how instruction works, to be effective in his or her unique setting. (Smagorinsky, 2010, p. 21)

We have worked in schools that have appropriate resources and generally supportive parents and administrators. Most of our students come to school sufficiently nourished, well rested, and secure. Few of these students found themselves navigating between radically different cultures and discourse communities when they left home and came to school. But we have also worked in schools where the conditions for learning and teaching are quite different. In these schools, we have engaged a wide range of learners in similar learning activities, with similar results. Smagorinsky's insights should alert all teachers to consider the special qualities and needs of the learners in their own classrooms when they attempt inquiry-based simulations that are potentially rich with opportunities for dialogue. The assumptions that we make about prior knowledge and about ways to discuss problems may be inaccurate or not shared. The controversy that students can approach with a cool detachment in one school might be emotionally charged in another, and the teacher will need to be aware of this possibility. Perhaps a teacher might find herself altering a simulation activity extensively, or providing a series of preparatory experiences that introduce students into the kind of dialogue that legislative hearings and town hall meetings require. The alterations might include adaptation of the texts, establishing supportive peer groups through strategic selection of members, sharing graphic representations of the sequence of activities, modeling the group work and the large-group deliberations, and modeling the process of taking notes and working from notes to compose more cohesive reports and narratives.

We hope that this chapter has offered an appropriate theory and research foundation for the materials that we share in the book. The chapters that follow depict students in action—as experts testifying before a legislative committee, as participants in town hall meetings, and as war-weary travelers returning home from Appomattox. The activities rely on features that make them attractive to most learners: They engage in problem solving of the sort that leaders faced throughout U.S. history, they work frequently with peers, they assume imagined identities for the temporary pleasure of the game, they have clear purpose for their reading and writing, and they know immediately where they have been successful and where they need to improve their own efforts to advance the play. We expect that the following pages will introduce you to learners in action and engrossed in their learning, and we are confident that teachers from middle school through high school can imitate or adapt the models to construct similar activities for their own learners.

CHAPTER 1

Looking for Repairs in Our Daily Lives

A school administrator pounded a gavel at a table in the school library, calling to order a simulated legislative hearing. At the table with the administrator sat a parent, a professor from a local university, and a graduate student from the same university. These participants came to the classroom as invitees prepared to play a role, coached in the forum protocol and prepared to gently grill the student experts who offered their testimonies. The administrator, serving as chair of the "legislative committee," called on a panel of experts to testify about the Cherokee Nation—how and where they lived, their experiences with the new settlers from Europe—and to offer their opinion about reparations owed to the tribe because of the harms done at the hands of the settlers. When called on by the chair, a student named Eric offered this "expert" testimony:

> A man named John G. Burnett wrote a letter to his children on his birthday in 1890 describing the horrible journey, now called the Trail of Tears. He was a private in the army at the time. In his letter he told that he "witnessed the execution of the most brutal order in the history of American Warfare." He saw helpless Cherokees arrested and dragged from homes and driven at bayonet point into the temporary jails set up to hold them. On the journey, there was bad cold weather. Burnett wrote, "This trail of the exiles was a trail of death." Cherokees didn't have enough food or blankets or clothing. He recalled as many as 22 Cherokees died "in one night of pneumonia due to ill treatment, cold and exposure." Burnett witnessed a man using a whip on an old and nearly blind Cherokee man. He stopped it at risk to himself.
>
> About 4,000 people died on this Trail of Tears from the foothills of the Smoky Mountains to what became Oklahoma.
>
> As you have heard from others today, reservation life was difficult for all Native American tribes. The mission to "civilize" the Cherokee resulted in the slow loss of Cherokee way of life and culture. Missionaries sought to convert the Cherokee to Christianity and taught the Cherokee English, instead of encouraging use of their native Cherokee language. The sense of Cherokee community was splintering away as generations were losing a sense of traditions and culture.

It's hard to ask for reparations for wrongs done a long time ago. Just because it's hard doesn't mean it shouldn't be tried. A sincere apology from today's government with an acknowledgment of these injustices would be a good start. The Cherokee should get some land back to call their own—land that is rich in natural resources and can be farmed, for those Cherokee today who would like to farm. For those that live on reservations, the government should consider funding for better homes and job opportunities. For all Cherokee, scholarships could help reverse the damage to our people. The poverty cycle of the reservation Cherokee needs to end.

Eric was a member of a team of students who set out to gather information about one group of Native Americans to report to a committee of "legislators" in a simulated legislative hearing. Eric and his partners had done much to prepare for their testimony through their research, their organization of assembled stories and information, and their negotiation of the parts they would play before the panel. Their report to the committee was both the end of an inquiry process and the preparation for an elaborated written response.

When we embarked on a collaborative effort to look for ways to integrate writing instruction into a jam-packed curriculum, we saw potential in social studies units, which offered a narrow survey of U.S. history, mostly in the form of a straightforward narrative that raised few debatable question. The history curriculum began with a unit about "the first Americans," but the textbook treatment of Native Americans was more somnolent than inspiring. While we saw importance in students learning about Native Americans, we sought an authentic gateway into the subject—a way to infuse purpose into reading, writing, and talking about Native Americans. We settled on the concept of *reparations*. While the legal and ethical concept is abstract and complicated, it is hardly remote from students' own experience and appeals directly to their preoccupation with fair treatment and their recognition of the need for penalties for wrongdoing. One of the appeals of the line of inquiry was that students would be able to talk from a position of some expertise about a policy question that continues to be a debatable issue in contemporary society.

LOOKING AHEAD AND PLANNING BACKWARD

We envisioned that students would eventually be able to write intelligently about whether or not the United States should provide reparations for Native American tribes that suffered various harms caused by the incursions of European settlers, and later sustained and sometimes extended by the

U.S. government. Furthermore, we anticipated that students would become involved in discussions about reparations and their research about particular victims of oppression would equip them to think about the appeals for reparations for any oppressed people. We asked students to consider this supposition: A member of the legislature has proposed a bill that requires the U.S. government to provide reparations for several Native American tribes. As part of the legislative process, the sponsor of the bill has organized hearings to allow experts to testify about the experiences of the Native Americans and to offer their opinions about possible reparations. The information gathered at the hearing would inform the bill and could influence and garner support from the members of a committee that would decide if the bill moved forward in the process of making a proposed bill law. In the end, the central question was this: What, if anything, should legislators do to compensate Native American tribes and to make amends for harms to a whole group of people?

Our end goal was to elicit informed, elaborated, and lucid responses to this guiding question from students. Of course, there was much to do to move the learners toward this goal. We recognized that before the students considered the questions about a proposed reparations bill, they would need experience with two preliminary efforts: (1) Define the "rules" for *reparations* (i.e., criteria for judging when reparations are appropriate, and the form they should take) and (2) apply the "rules" in deciding a local case of oppression. Table 1.1 projects the entire sequence and suggests what a teacher might look for as an outcome before proceeding from one phase of the sequence to another.

A NOTE ABOUT ASSESSMENT

We offer below and in the subsequent chapters a series of learning activities that led to students producing some remarkable writing. The students' letters, essays, and narratives revealed to us not only their command of various forms of written composition and their knowledge about important concepts about U.S. history. We based our assessment on three considerations: (1) how students measured up to the performance expectations expressed in the Common Core Learning Standards (see Appendix C for a rubric for writing), (2) how students performed against the standards of the C3 Framework for learning in social studies, and (3) how students compared to a proficiency standard suggested to us by the performance of students at the same grade in the same school in the past.

We have also found it useful to collect a baseline writing sample early in the school year. We offer students several prompts that we judge as tasks similar to those that students tackle later in the school year. Appendix A

Table 1.1. Overview of the Reparations Sequence

Phase	Actions	Outcomes
I. Defining the concept of *reparations* and setting guidelines for invoking and managing reparations.	• In small groups, students discuss their decisions about reparations for the victims depicted in a set of scenarios ("You Be the Judge"). • As a whole class, students suggest criteria for reparations and offer arguments to support or illustrate each criterion statement.	Collaboratively, the students *express several criteria* for judging when reparations are necessary and for deciding the form and extent of the repairs. Having constructed a set of criteria, the students have a *critical framework for judging cases* when oppressed people appeal for reparations.
II. Applying the criteria to a school-based situation.	• Drawing on the criteria for judging reparations, students work in small groups to judge how a victim should be compensated. • In a whole-class forum, students share their arguments for the appropriate compensatory actions that bullies should provide for their victim.	Each student writes *a letter to a school principal* to recall a cycle of bullying and to argue for a specific course of reparations, citing the details of the case and the criteria for judging the need and form of reparations.
III. Preparing for testimony	• Students work in teams to research a specific Native American tribe or a community of early settlers, noting the distinctive qualities of the tribe's culture and the harms that the tribe suffered as a result of the arrival of European settlers. • Students share their individual findings to coordinate a report to a legislative committee.	Collaboratively, teams of students compose presentations to share as testimony before the simulated legislative hearing.
IV. Testifying before a legislative committee	• Each team presents testimony about an individual tribe or about a community of settlers. • Students respond to questions from the team of "legislators," clarifying their testimony and arguing for or against reparations. • Students note all the testimonies and the question-and-answer exchanges in order to expand their knowledge about harms, reprisals, and complications.	Students compose *a letter to a legislative leader* to argue for or against a proposed reparations bill, citing testimony across the teams and applying the criteria for judging the need and appropriate form for reparations.

offers examples of the prompts for the baseline sample. The comparison of compositions from early and late in the school year allow us a summary picture of students' growth as writers.

We also rely on less formal means for assessment. What students say in class reveals to us their recall of events in history, their analysis of events (especially causal relationships), their skills at arguments about policy questions, their attentiveness to the contributions of their peers, and their general management of the protocols for civil discourse. Appendix B offers a rubric for assessing students through their contributions to discussions.

DEFINING THE CONCEPT OF *REPARATIONS*

As with many occasions for argument, the evaluation of the proposed reparations bill depends on a definition of an abstract concept. Several writers (Hillocks, 2011; Hillocks, Kahn, & Johannessen, 1983; Smagorinsky, Johannessen, Kahn, & McCann, 2011) remind us that the recognition of specific criteria (e.g., characteristics of a *hero*, definition of a crime, features of *courageous action*, etc.) allows someone to judge if something in question meets an identified standard. To use Toulmin's (2000) term, the criteria from the definition can serve as the *warrants* that are useful for interpreting the significance of some information or example and connecting it to a claim.

While we recognized that the concept of *reparations* is abstract, it is not foreign to students' experience, and we judged that if we presented learners with a set of problem situations from which they could draw using personal experience and emerging understandings of ethical standards, they could talk productively about their decisions and collaboratively construct a kind of definition of the concept. The definition would take the form of a set of criterion statements that the students could then apply during their deliberations about more complicated and perhaps less familiar problems.

We prompted discussion through a series of scenarios, presenting everyday situations that the students might have experienced themselves or could well imagine. Each scenario presents a problem and asks the reader to decide what characters should do. Students readily decide in most cases, but the important effort is their expression of a standard or principle that would guide their decision. The problematic nature of the scenarios fosters both disagreement and dialogue. We scaffolded the scenarios by increasing levels of complexity, giving students some initial confidence that they could tackle the problems and then fostering an appreciation for the complexity of the issues. When we put students in a position to talk about the differences in their judgments, they work on *procedures for defining* and they discover the rules that would guide decisions about reparations.

In constructing the scenarios, we had to do our own research and keep in mind the various historical situations and the common arguments about reparations: What harms call for repairs? Who can be held responsible? How can you repair something that seems an irreparable harm? Is there a statute of limitations? Are token gestures enough? Should repairs be both compensatory and punitive?

We offer the set of scenarios below, followed by examples of students' discussions about the scenarios. The first scenario appears also in *Transforming Talk into Text* (McCann, 2014), but the remaining scenarios offer new possibilities to prompt the discussion that generates the criteria to guide decisionmaking.

If the discussions based on scenarios are a new practice for students, we recommend that the teacher model the facilitation of discussion by leading the deliberation about the first scenario. Serving as the facilitator, the teacher can help students with the wording of their sense of principles and record the consensus across the class. Ideally, the teacher models the inclusion of all willing contributors and asks the appropriate follow-up questions to press students to clarify their thinking and express logical arguments in defense of proposed criterion statements.

YOU BE THE JUDGE: FOUR SITUATIONS FOR YOU TO CONSIDER

What are the appropriate reparations?

1. During a dispute about the use of a friend's jump rope, 8-year-old Stella Jenkins bit her neighbor, 7-year-old Lucy Madison. The bite on Lucy's forearm hurt very much, drew a little blood, and left Lucy in tears. After Lucy reported the incident to her mother, Mrs. Madison brought Lucy back to the Jenkins home, described the scene to Mrs. Jenkins, and demanded an apology from Stella to Lucy. Reluctantly, Stella said, "Okay. I'm sorry. So there." Lucy was not satisfied. Her arm still hurt, and it would probably be bruised for days. Sufficiently traumatized by the attack, Lucy would remain afraid to play with Stella again. To what extent is the apology a satisfactory repair? If more reparations are necessary, what would you expect? If Stella has done all she could do, how would you explain this to Lucy?

2. When Tiburcio Herrerra began 3rd grade at Roosevelt School, Mrs. Whitehall, his new teacher, awkwardly pronounced his name during roll call and said, "That's a mouthful. To simplify things, we'll call you Timmy around here. That should make you feel more comfortable around your new classmates." Later that same day, Mrs. Whitehall directed Tiburcio to hide under his shirt the small crucifix that hung from a chain down the front of his T-shirt. "This is not a religious school, so we will not display religious symbols." She also corrected Tiburcio several times by directing him not to speak any Spanish in

class. Tiburcio thereafter became known only as Timmy in school and spoke Spanish only occasionally at home. He eventually lost his original Spanish fluency and sense of pride in his language and its ties to his Mexican heritage. Years later, when Tiburcio returned to the neighborhood of Roosevelt School, he felt compelled to confront Mrs. Whitehall. What, if anything, could the young man now called Timmy demand of Mrs. Whitehall? How, if at all, had she damaged Tiburcio, and what could she do about it?

3. At the time that Wilbert Cousins returned from his army service during World War I, he discovered that a local merchant had bought Wilbert's dry goods store at a bargain price from the aunt to whom Wilbert had trusted its care. Aunt Zelda was quite old at the time, and the merchant, Vance Simms, had convinced her that Wilbert had died in combat and would never return, leaving her in need of relief from running a business and money to secure a comfortable retirement. With the addition of the profitable store to his holdings, Vance Simms became the dominant economic power in the town. For his part, Wilbert returned from war physically limited from his battle wounds, married, had children, and eked out a living with a succession of temporary jobs. Bolstered by his financial gains at the cost of Wilbert's losses, Vance Simms married and started a family of his own. His children went to fancy boarding schools and prestigious universities, with educations and contacts that launched them into a life of privilege. Now Wilbert Cousins's great-grandchildren, in an attempt to raise themselves out of poverty, have examined the original agreement on the sale of the store and are seeking fair compensation from the Vance family. What can they expect from the descendants of Vance Simms when his great-grandchildren claim that they had never done the Cousins any wrong? To what extent are these descendants still responsible for repairing the damage their great-grandfather had caused? What form, if anything, would this repair take?

4. When the Japanese attack on Pearl Harbor launched the United States into World War II, many Americans worried that Japanese Americans living in the United States, even those who were born in the United States and were far removed from Japanese language and culture, might find themselves more loyal to Japan than to the United States. These irrational suspicions ultimately caused President Franklin D. Roosevelt to issue an order to have Japanese and Japanese Americans rounded up and sent to camps far away from their homes. During this time, their property was confiscated and in many instances sold to others at bargain prices. Many of these citizens, some of whom had family members serving with distinction in the war, could never recover their property. In one instance, the Manzanar family moved into a Seattle home once owned and occupied by the Takata family. The Takatas

received no compensation. Now members of the Takata family want to reclaim the house and displace the current generation of the Manzanar family. What claims do the Takatas have on the old house? Must the Manzanars surrender the house with no payment for it?

TEACHER-MODELED DISCUSSION

After the teacher read the first scenario aloud, she invited students to share their recommendations and the reasons behind their decisions. The teacher's "moves" included paraphrasing rather than judging the responses, inviting students to evaluate one another's recommendations, and asking follow-up questions to urge students to express a kind of argument—the report of a decision, based on a rule, drawn from the scenario and comparable situations.

> *Ms. D'Angelo:* So, in this situation, is Stella saying that she is sorry enough? Will Lucy and her mother think that this is enough? Lauren, what do you think?
>
> *Lauren:* I would want her to actually mean it when she apologizes.
>
> *Brett:* I think Stella should say sorry and actually give her something like candy or something added to show that she was really sorry.
>
> *Milan:* How do you make someone give a sincere apology?
>
> *Allison:* I think that Lucy can explain how she feels to be bitten. Explain it hurt and hurt her feelings.
>
> *Evan:* She needs to know the golden rule.
>
> *Milan:* You cannot make someone feel different. You want them to apologize on their own.
>
> *Gracie:* There should be a punishment by not playing with Lucy for a long time. Then Stella will get lonely and miss her and want to apologize to be friends again.
>
> *Tom:* Should Lucy be allowed to bite Stella?
>
> *Milan:* Well, you don't want Lucy to become like Stella and Stella to feel the same way toward Lucy.
>
> *Ms. D'Angelo:* So it sounds like the guiding principle here is that if someone hurts someone else, the offender should offer a genuine apology. You also want the offender to do something a little extra to make up for hurting someone. Is that right?

We have found that the teacher's modeling has a powerful influence on the students' conduct in their small groups. When the students moved into small groups, they tackled a few of the scenarios at a time, with each requiring a good deal of discussion. We show a typical example of a small-group discussion below and list the criteria that one class compiled as "rules" for determining when reparations are necessary and what form they should take.

SMALL-GROUP TALK

In one class, Ms. D'Angelo organized students into groups of four. She then explained that the students were to discuss specific scenarios and suggested a time limit for the discussion. Ms. D'Angelo was careful to note that she didn't necessarily expect the students to agree but she wanted them to try to arrive at consensus, while noting exceptions. She also emphasized that the outcome of the discussion would be a list of "rules" that would be used to guide decisions in more complicated situations. The exchange below shows students tackling the tough situation represented in scenario 3 (Cousins vs. Simms).

> *Brett:* They should pay back the money that the guy cheated the grandfather out of.
> *Clark:* And it has to be a lot more than the store was worth a long time ago. If that store was worth like $10,000 during World War I, that has to be like five times that now.
> *Ms. D'Angelo:* So, if you inherited something that was gained dishonestly, are you responsible?
> *Clark:* Yes.
> *Ava:* You must do something to help the Cousins family because they could have been rich, but the Simms guy made them all poor.
> *Gracie:* The Simms should give the Cousins a fair amount.
> *Devon:* They got their money because their grandfather cheated the old aunt. It is not like they stole money themselves, but they got good educations and good jobs because their great-grandfather did.
> *Evan:* He didn't really steal, but he tricked them.
> *Allison:* If the Simms help the Cousins, they can all be better off.
> *Milan:* Yeah. The Simms shouldn't become poor like the Cousins.

This excerpt from a more extended conversation reveals students grappling with familiar arguments about the compensation for people who historically have been oppressed as a group. As the students struggled with this dilemma, they concluded that the beneficiaries of wrongdoing owe something to the victims so that the latter have an opportunity to advance their lot in life.

After the small-group work, Ms. D'Angelo facilitated the debriefing with the entire class. To be frank, the small-group conversations and large-group debriefing is a prolonged process, but one that pays off with the collaborative construction of a critical framework that is necessary for proceeding to the next phases in the inquiry sequence. Here are the rules that members of one class derived through their discussions:

- If someone hurts someone else, the person who does the harm should offer a sincere apology.

- If someone damages an item belonging to someone else, the person who caused the damage should pay to have it fixed or replaced to the satisfaction of the harmed person.
- In correcting a person for doing harm, the punishment should teach a lesson and not just hurt the person.
- Some damages cannot be fixed with just money or replacing an item. In this case, pay the person back as best as possible and do a kind act that shows thoughtful concern for the loss.
- Financial compensation should be as least as much or maybe more than that which is owed and it should take into account losses that have nothing to do with money.
- If government officials or representatives of the government do harm, the current government officials must provide compensation to the satisfaction of the harmed person(s) no matter how much time has elapsed from the original incident.

As the teacher discussed students' decisions and heard their arguments, she helped with the wording but checked with the students that she was representing them accurately and to their satisfaction. She might have entered the discussion with "rules" of her own, but she trusted in the inquiry process and remained confident that the students would express some reasonable criteria and that the learners would internalize the conclusions that they discovered together.

APPLYING THE RULES TO A NEW CASE

Before the students would tackle the simulated legislative hearing about a proposed bill for Native American reparations, which we describe in Chapter 2, we wanted students to tackle a more local, and in ways parallel, situation. We anticipated that the 5th-graders, who would soon move on to the middle school, would be sensitive to issues about bullying. The bully's oppression of a middle school victim and the systematic harms to Native Americans are not exactly parallel. The obvious difference is the scope of the problem. But we wanted to put the students in the position to apply the rules that they derived and, through their discussions and writing, practice with the procedures for writing an argument in response to a policy question (e.g., what action should we take in regard to a given problem?). We purposely structured the two prompts (i.e., the school-based bully situation and the Native American reparations bill) in a similar way so that we would have a basis for judging students' progress as writers as they moved from a self-contained case to a broader problem that required independent and shared research and use of the distributed expertise across a class of peers.

We recommend that the work with the case should follow at least three stages: individual preparation, consultation with partners, and whole-class discussion. As we have come to understand from observing the work of a variety of teachers (McCann, 2014), each stage has its distinct function in the process of preparation for writing. Students come to small-group work with something to say about the case. The group work allows students to try out their opinions on others and hear other possibilities and perspectives. In small groups there are likely to be some disagreements, which put students in a position to support their judgments and perhaps reframe their thinking. After the small-group work, students come to the large group with developed arguments. The large-group work showcases a variety of arguments, which each participant evaluates and draws from in order to elaborate on them in the letter to the principal.

In the middle school bully case, a brother-and-sister team (Leila and Landon) have harassed a classmate in a number of ways. Here are some examples of the harms done by the bullies to the victim, Jimmy:

- Stole lunch money from him, leaving him on many days with nothing to eat for lunch.
- Hit him and twisted his arm in a painful position when he resisted giving up his lunch money.
- Took his graphing calculator for their own use, causing Jimmy to get into trouble with his math teacher for forgetting to bring the calculator to class.
- Called him many insulting names in front of other students.
- Teased him about wearing a Cubs jersey, because they were Cardinals fans and hated the Cubs.
- Threatened to beat him up if he wore any Cubs clothing to school, scaring Jimmy into never wearing the emblem of his favorite team again.
- Took a picture of Jimmy when it looked like he was picking his nose on the playground and posted the picture on a website that invited viewers to write cruel comments.
- Wrote nasty rumors about him on the website, including the claim that he had a crush on Mrs. Zeeler, the ancient library assistant at the school.

A fuller account of the case appears in McCann (2014); however, the essential features of the case are that a victim has reported how he has been harmed and observers like our students are left to judge how significant his suffering has been and what actions the bullies might be influenced to take in an effort to repair the harms.

DISCUSSION ABOUT THE CASE

After the class read the case narrative together and reviewed the details about the case, Becky (Ms. D'Angelo) asked her students to talk in groups of three or four about what they thought would be appropriate steps to try to repair the damage done to Jimmy. The following composite of exchanges is representative of the kind of interactions we have seen among students across several years.

> *Ms. D'Angelo:* Now that you have had a chance to talk about Jimmy's case in your groups, I'm interested in knowing what you think the principal should do and what Leila and Landon can do.
>
> *Sheila:* I don't know if the principal can make them do anything. I mean, Leila is already in high school and doesn't go to that school anymore.
>
> *Raphael:* I know what they should do. They've got to give everything back.
>
> *Ms. D'Angelo:* Give what back?
>
> *Raphael:* Well, they took his lunch money, and they took his calculator.
>
> *Ms. D'Angelo:* Those things obviously sound bad, but why is taking the money and the calculator especially harmful? How is Jimmy hurt by those actions?
>
> *Connor:* It was his lunch money. He had to go a lot of days without anything to eat for lunch. I am hungry right now. I imagine that he was starving if he had to go the whole day without anything to eat.
>
> *Brandon:* And he got in trouble about the calculator because his math teacher thought that he kept forgetting it.
>
> *Francesca:* The worst thing is that they took a picture of him picking his nose and they put that and a lot of insulting comments on a website. They even made up rumors that he had a crush on the very old library aide.
>
> *Ms. D'Angelo:* How is that the *worst* thing? Is that worse than hitting him or twisting his arm, which can really hurt?
>
> *Mia:* Jimmy doesn't know who is looking at the picture and the comments. The whole world could be looking at it and laughing at it. It is bigger because it could be the whole world.
>
> *Ms. D'Angelo:* Okay. I am beginning to appreciate the damage. What else did you decide?
>
> *Melina:* They have to apologize. That was like our first rule: If you hurt someone, you have to apologize. And it has to be a sincere apology.
>
> *Ms. D'Angelo:* Do you want them to apologize just to Jimmy?
>
> *Joyce:* They don't have to apologize to the whole school or anything. They didn't really hurt anyone except Jimmy.
>
> *Connor:* We don't know if they did this stuff to other kids.

Joyce: Well, we don't know, so it would be unfair to apologize to everyone, like they hurt everyone in the school.

This excerpt from a longer discussion shows students' efforts during oral discourse to make a case for reparation action for Jimmy's sake.

We also see students invoking the rules that they constructed during early discussions. From witnessing these many discussions and from an earlier report (McCann, 2014), we concluded that students began to internalize a critical voice that suggests what a skeptical audience might be thinking and might require in the way of support for claims and rules for guiding policy. We offer below one example of a student's subsequent written response to the case.

WRITTEN RESPONSE TO THE CASE

After our extensive discussions, we prompted the students to write to the school principal to advise him about what should be done in this case. To draft the letter to the principal, the students drew from notes made during class discussions and from the printed material about the case. We typically ask students to draft a response quickly and then share with the classroom teacher, with a teaching assistant, or with one another. We rely on the rubric that appears in Appendix C as a shared sense of the traits that should appear in the written response and as language for discussing elements of writing that is well done, in need of improvement, or missing entirely. The written and oral feedback on the drafts guides students in revising their efforts.

We offer Francesca's letter below as a typical example of a response to advise the principal. Francesca agrees with us that the letter leaves room for improvement, but she was generous enough to let us share her early writing, flaws and all.

Student's Letter to a Principal

Dear Dr. Philoman,

My name is Francesca and I heard about the bullying problem at Joseph Hill Middle School. I have some ideas that might help.

Some of the troubles that happened to Jimmy are that Landon and Leila stole his lunch money and left him with no lunch. Also, they wrote nasty rumors about Jimmy on a website. I think that is the worst because everyone in the world could see it. Next, Landon and Leila threatened to beat Jimmy up if he wore any Cubs apparel to school. Jimmy loved the Cubs, it was his favorite team. Last, they called him insulting names in front of other students. This has been happening since 3rd grade, they are now in 8th grade. This has been going on for too long and we need to put a stop to it.

I picked three of the most important punishments for Landon and Leila. The first punishment is removing all of the harmful and insulting material from the website. That punishment is fair because everyone in the world could see it and make fun of it without Jimmy knowing who they are. That is called cyber bullying. The second punishment is giving back all of Jimmy's stolen lunch money, plus a little extra. That punishment is fair because Jimmy didn't have anything to eat for several days. The last punishment is completing 100 hours of community service each by making anti-bullying posters and by talking to church youth groups about the harms of bullying. That punishment is fair because they will learn all about why bullying is bad and why it is important that we don't bully anybody.

Here are some other punishments that Jimmy's parents thought of but weren't as meaningful as those other three punishments. Buying Jimmy a new graphing calculator isn't fair because it couldn't really help him, they could just bully him after they give it back. Next, apologizing to Jimmy in front of his classmates isn't fair because his classmates could make fun of him. Also apologizing to the current and former students who witnessed the abuse to Jimmy isn't fair because, like before, students could make fun of him. Then, wearing Cubs apparel for several days is not fair because that won't stop Landon and Leila from bullying him. Last, buying Jimmy a new Cubs jersey is not fair because they never really stole it from him.

I think Landon and Leila were very bad and I hope they learn their lessons.

Sincerely,
Francesca

We were encouraged by Francesca's response. Experience tells us that Francesca's effort is quite lucid and elaborated for a 5th-grader. In this instance, we would have preferred that the student introduce the letter by briefly framing the problem for the principal's attention and that she demonstrate the impact the harm had on Jimmy so that the principal could judge whether reparations were necessary and what form they should take. But we recognize that this one piece of writing represents a stage in a broader process of development. In addition, the letter would benefit from some careful editing. If a teacher judged that it is important to refine the writing at this stage, the related rubric (see Appendix C) could guide peers in offering feedback or as a basis for conversation between the teacher and the writer. Less important than the refinement of the current composition is the idea that Francesca can move on to other occasions for writing, equipped with the procedures that she needs to advance logical arguments and weigh the arguments of others. We see that the current attempt in writing about a fairly narrow case with a limited body of information places Francesca and her classmates in a position to tackle a more complex problem, as we show in the next chapter.

LEARNING OUTCOMES FOR THE REPARATIONS SEQUENCE: A COMMON CORE "BONANZA"

The sequence that we describe in this chapter and extend into Chapter 2 requires a good deal of preparation and class time. Some teachers might question the investment of time in such a sequence. Part of our justification is that we trust that the inquiry process allows students to command complex procedures and deepen their understanding of concepts at the core of a discipline. We think the combination of the preparation described in this chapter, with the next phase described in Chapter 2, integrates a lot of learning, giving students experiences with the seamless combination of speaking, listening, reading, writing, researching, critical thinking, collaborating, and understanding eras of U.S. history and the lasting legacy of our national forebears. In other words, the wealth of learning actually makes the process more efficient than the notoriously inefficient attempt to transmit knowledge that students do not internalize and cannot use to build on. We have seen time and again, as in the scenario discussion reported earlier in the chapter, that students not only construct knowledge for use in the subsequent activity but are also positioned to enter into contemporary debates about the kind of complex political issues that many would assume to be adult conversation.

During a conference presentation where we shared the material from this chapter and Chapter 2, one participant noted that the sequence of learning experiences represented a "Common Core bonanza." We find the comment both funny and a source of pride. The next chapter shows the payoff for the extensive preparation as students move away from the fictionalized scenarios and case to historical events in which real humans suffered real harm, requiring thoughtful responses to the calls for accepting responsibility.

CHAPTER 2

Legislative Hearing: Inquiry into Reparations

As we share in Chapter 1, even when a simulated legislative hearing gives students an opportunity to "play" in roles as adults, that play requires a good deal of preparation. By the time students enter into the simulated world of a legislative process, they have defined an abstract concept, applied the criteria of the definition in assessing the behavior of characters and arguing for a policy, worked collaboratively on several occasions, and participated in civil conversations with their peers about matters that they cared about. These experiences equipped students with many of the procedures that they would need to testify at a legislative hearing and respond to questions from a committee of legislators. Of course, no committee would invite guests to testify unless those invitees had some expertise to contribute to the legislators' understanding of the issues related to a proposed action. This means that students would have built their knowledge about specific tribes or non-Native settlers to North America to attain "expert" status. The next step, then, is for students to work in teams to research a particular tribe or representative settlement and combine their distributed understandings to a group report to present to the committee.

We offer below the directions that students receive, followed by a description of the collaborative research process. We end the chapter with samples of the learners in action and an example of a student's written response to the sponsor of the reparations bill. Here is a brief overview of the process that we have followed:

1. Introduce the problem.
2. Assign teams, based on an assessment of learner characteristics.
3. Plan, prompt, and complete research (librarian help).
4. Teams submit a brief (draft of a report to the legislative committee).
5. Select panelists to present to the committee.
6. Conduct hearing.
7. Deliberate about policy/law.
8. Teams revise and submit a written report.
9. Individuals write to advise the sponsor of the reparations bill.

This overview focuses on the steps in the simulated legislative hearing, but there are two extensions. We want students to draw from the various testimonies and reports to see the broad picture so they can judge for themselves, not as imagined characters, whether or not to support a reparations bill—not just for Native Americans but for any exploited or abused peoples. For the sake of the simulation, the students support an assigned viewpoint as they testify as experts. Constructing their own report and responding to the questions from legislators fosters one level of thinking about the problem, but we also include all the students in a broader conversation about the sense they make about all they have heard. As they think about the harms endured by Native Americans and settlers, they judge if reparations are appropriate and propose what form the repairs might take. The large-group discussion measures the wisdom and viability of the proposed bill and individual written responses to the issues. In time, with further reading and other discussions, students judge the wisdom and justice of offering some form of reparation for others—such as African Americans, Japanese Americans, or survivors of various attempts at genocide or their descendants. We have seen evidence in students' discussion and writing that they have developed procedures for judging other contemporary situations (e.g., when a group of people have been systematically excluded from decent housing) when victims have called for repairs.

THE LANGUAGE OF THE CASE

The descriptions about the problem at the heart of the inquiry and the directions for students' collaborations, participation, and written responses include some vocabulary that might be new to students. The newness, of course, depends on the grade and the development of the learners. The subject is a mature one, and discussants typically use some advanced vocabulary to talk about the issues. Each teacher would have to judge how familiar a specific group of learners would be with a set of vocabulary. Instead of dodging potentially difficult language, we choose to introduce it to the students as part of our talk in the classroom, and we help students to figure out meanings by recognizing how a word is used in a specific context.

We also turn students' attention to the abstract academic vocabulary that tells students what they are expected to do, such as draw from their research, explain the significance, recommend action, rely on guidelines, and summarize. Presumably the language prompts students' actions and production so that the teachers can observe and make inferences about students' proficiencies and development. We rely heavily on modeling procedures to demonstrate how to support claims, interpret the significance of information, refer to established criteria, and so on. We encourage students to ask questions for clarification, but we mostly monitor actions and intervene with further clarifications and modeling when the directions appear to be unclear to some students.

LEGISLATIVE HEARING:
AN INQUIRY INTO POSSIBLE REPARATIONS
FOR NATIVE AMERICAN TRIBES

Background: Members of the legislature have been considering requests for a bill to provide reparations for several Native American tribes. If passed, the bill would become a law that requires the government to make amends for past harms to Native American tribes. The tribes claim that they have been harmed financially, physically, culturally, and socially. Not everyone likes the idea of the bill. Some people point to the harms that Native Americans inflicted on settlers from Europe and deny that the tribes deserve any reparations.

It is common for a committee of the legislature to conduct a hearing to collect information before anyone attempts to write a bill. The purpose of the current hearing is to find answers to the following questions:

- Has anyone been hurt?
- If someone has been hurt, how significant or bad was the injury?
- Has anything already been done to correct the injury and to make sure that it doesn't occur again?
- What should be done to repair the injury? Why should this action be taken? (How do these actions meet the "rules" for reparations?)
- How will the new actions help?

Preparation: Before legislators can hold a hearing, they have to find people who are knowledgeable about the subject of their hearing. In this case, they have to rely on people who know about the history of the tribes and the history of the settlers who came into contact with the tribes. In other words, the committee members want to hear from a group of experts.

In order to gather the information that will be the focus for the hearing, teams of investigators need to research the following groups (or another list of tribes affected by incursions from non-Native settlers):

- Powhatan
- Mohawk
- Delaware (Lenni Lenape)
- Cherokee
- Sioux
- Early settlers (New England, New York, and Pennsylvania)

Research assistants and the legislative librarian will help each team to find information about the tribes and the early settlers. Each team will gather information in order to *write a report* to *present at a hearing* and will need to *be prepared to answer questions* from the legislators on the committee.

Here is what your team will need to find out:

1. *Life of the tribe or settlement*: Where and how did the tribe or the settlers live? What were the language and the key elements in the culture of the tribe or settlement? What made the group distinctive? How can you convince people who think of the early tribes as "primitive" that the tribes actually had advanced societies?

2. *First encounters*: What were the first encounters between Native American and settlers like? To what extent did they initially live peacefully and in support of each other?

3. *Evidence of abuse*: What evidence do you have that settlers caused harm to the tribe, or that tribes caused harm to the settlers? To what extent were people hurt physically? To what extent were people hurt financially, including through the loss of land? To what extent did people lose some elements of the way they liked to live (e.g., language, customs, ties to a particular place)? In the end, how can you demonstrate that people suffered significantly?

4. *Calculation of repairs*: Considering the established guidelines for reparations, what do you recommend for reparations for a particular group, if any?

5. *Answers to questions*: What questions do you think that the legislative committee might have for you? How can you answer the questions that you expect to be asked?

After your team has collected the necessary information, your team will need to produce a *written report*. You can look at the *sample report* to give you an idea of what your report should look like. When the legislative hearing begins, someone from your team will read your team's report out loud, or you can take turns in presenting the parts of your report. Everyone on your team should be prepared to answer questions.

Procedures for the Hearing: At least one person from each team will present to the legislative committee for your team. There will be a legislative committee chair, who will set the agenda and direct the actions of the legislative committee. Here is the general agenda:

1. Opening of meeting and expression of goal
2. Testimony (reading written statement) and questions and answers
3. Questions and reactions from legislative committee members
4. Vote to recommend reparations after all teams have testified

Written Report: After the hearing, each team will reconvene to revise and refine the team's written report. The various reports during the hearing and the answers to questions are likely to provide more information to include in the team's final report. When all the reports are completed, they will be available to everyone.

COLLABORATIVE RESEARCH

In order for students to play at being experts testifying before a committee of legislators, they need to develop their expertise. We have formed teams of three or four students and assigned them each to research a particular tribe or a community of settlers. When we organize groups for this project and for the examples described in other chapters, we try to achieve a mix that is both supportive and diverse. For example, we want each group to include confident, outspoken members and more diffident members. When a student is an English language learner or might experience other challenges in understanding the materials and the team's task, we try to embed students who are likely to be supportive and perhaps patient. In brief, the formation of the groups is strategic and requires knowing a class of students well.

Each team is tasked with researching and producing a report that it can present to the legislative panel. While "research" in the sense of looking up information and taking some notes is not entirely new to our students, finding accessible and appropriate online and print resources for the purposes of the simulation has presented some challenges. Specifically, the difficulty is in finding accessible, reliable, and unbiased accounts of Native American interaction with European settlers through the years.

We caution teachers about some possible difficulties and recommend ways for students to find, compile, and organize information in order to share expertise with a legislative committee at a public hearing. We wanted to direct students to compile specific kinds of information that would be appropriate for testimony before the legislative committee, but we did not want to deliver the research to the students. The device we have relied on to direct students' research is a letter to each team of "experts." The letter comes from a supporter who urges the team to make an informed and energetic case for reparations. While this letter suggests an approach for the research and urges advocacy for a particular point of view, the broader inquiry involves the consideration of all the testimonies and the subsequent questions and debate. The first concern is positioning students to be able to enter testimony into the record. We offer one example of an advocacy letter below. Other examples appear in Appendix D.

Dear Delegation Members,

I recognize that you will be appearing to offer expert testimony to the members of the legislative committee considering a bill for reparations for Native Americans. I trust that you will prepare for your appearance before the committee by researching the history of our people. I offer as a reminder that as a Nation of Native Peoples we have been victims of repeated harms, indignities, and deprivations. When you testify, please keep the following in mind:

- We have been driven from ancestral lands repeatedly when European settlers found value in the land that we occupied. I would invite the legislators to trace the "Trail of Tears" that ran from Georgia and North Carolina to Arkansas and later to the plains and western states. At least three presidents supported our removal and displacement—Monroe, Jefferson, and Jackson. *Please be prepared to tell the story of the Trail of Tears so that others know how we suffered. Refer to the story [i.e., birthday letter to his children] of Private John G. Burnett to know the poignant details of our suffering.*

- Leaders of the United States government betrayed us. Our support of General Jackson during the War of 1812 surely saved his command and probably saved his life, but he was personally responsible for displacing us to the western reaches of the United States and ignored our please for mercy. *Please be prepared to tell the story of our support of General Jackson and of his betrayal when he became president.*

- We have been repeatedly characterized as ignorant savages, with the dominant Eurocentric settlers claiming that we have *no government, no strong family values, a crude language, no fine arts, and no sense of civility.* In short, they claim that we have no culture at all. *Please be prepared to tell the story of our culture and offer examples of how our displacement threatened the total destruction of the many valuable aspects of our culture.*

- Many Eurocentric settlers depict us as pagans and infidels, with no religion except for a collection of superstitions and curious rituals. *Please be prepared to explain our system of faith and distinguish our rites and rituals from savage mutterings.*

- We have been cheated repeatedly with devious treaties or by the failure of the U.S. government to honor the treaties that we entered into in good faith. *Please be prepared to tell the story of how we were forced into treaties that caused us to surrender our lands and move to far less desirable environments.*

As John Burnett admitted in his letter of long ago, "Murder is murder, and somebody must answer." Perhaps the murderers are long gone, but someone must be held to account for the suffering of our people. *Be sure to tell our story completely, accurately, and compellingly.*

Respectfully,
John A. Ross

While the students had an advocacy letter to prompt their research and to suggest specific details to learn about in order to report, the teacher and school librarian monitored progress and provided assistance. The assistance came in the form of clarifying the research task, suggesting sources of information, and reacting to what students had discovered. As students gathered information from print and online sources, they shared the information they found and drew conclusions about what their findings revealed about the extent of harms and the implications for reparations. Here is an example of students at work in sharing information for their written report and oral testimony about the plight of the Cherokee Nation:

Sam: Lots of Cherokee people signed a treaty saying they are willing to give up their land to go to Oklahoma.

Jack: Yeah, but in return the U.S. would pay for a year's supply of food and give them something else.

Eric: They never did that. Some non-Native people wanted to give them what they needed.

Sam: Then the soldiers forced them to walk the whole time and gave them food that was rotten.

Jack: Lucky people had two blankets.

Eric: They didn't get the clothing they needed. It was cold.

Lexie: A lot of them didn't survive . . . about 3,000 people died.

Jack: It was normal for them to bury 14 people a day.

Sam: They had to leave because gold was discovered there and the government wanted the Natives out of the area. The Treaty of New Echota 1835 gave the U.S. all lands east of the Mississippi.

Jack: Gold was found in their territory and the White people wanted it.

Sam: The judicial people said the Native Americans could keep land but Andrew Jackson didn't let them.

Lexie: Not positive, but Andrew Jackson promised he . . .

Eric: The Cherokee helped Jackson out in a war.

Sam: In 1813 at the Battle of Horseshoe Bend.

Jack: The U.S. people were losing. They were no match for Tecumseh. Then all of a sudden from a river behind them the 800 Cherokees came and helped the U.S. defeat the Creek and Shawnee. They attacked from the rear.

Jack: Andrew Jackson and the government won the war because of the
   Cherokee's help.
Eric: Jackson promised them he would be good to them.
Sam: Twenty-five years later Jackson gets the chance to help them.
   The judicial people said that the Cherokee get to keep their land.
   Then Jackson said [finds quote], "John Marshall has rendered his
   decision; let him enforce it if he can." That was horrible that he
   didn't help them after they had helped the U.S. beat the Creek and
   Shawnee at Horseshoe Bend.

The conversation reveals that students have found and shared relevant information, but they also evaluated the significance of the information they found. The collaborative process reveals that the students both synthesized and evaluated information.

Not only did students gather information to share with a legislative committee; they also drew on their earlier expression of "rules" for reparations (Chapter 1) to recommend steps that the federal government might take to respond to the harms caused to a tribe in the past. Here is one team's discussion of possible reparations for the Sioux tribe:

Nino: I bet the Sioux would rather have a sincere apology instead of
   just money.
Niko: I don't get why they didn't take the $106 million they were
   offered before. They probably could have bought the Black Hills
   back with that.
Nicole: What would they do with the $106 million? They don't need
   it—they don't want it.
Nino: Something to give back to them . . .
Nicole: They should give them better land so they can actually grow
   something.
Niko: You could probably buy a whole state with that. It's better than
   nothing.
Evan: Instead of listening to the government telling them to go to
   Oklahoma, they could have gone more west, they could have gotten
   more land—
Nino: I think the Sioux today would feel better if they knew the
   government actually cared. At least an apology.
Nicole: The government should put them in Wisconsin, close to North
   Dakota and South Dakota, and don't cage them.
Evan: They should have fair rights. They should have people live like
   the Sioux on a reservation for one week and know what it feels
   like.
Nino: It was pretty much like the government walking up to your house
   saying you move here or we'll take it down.

While the students' research about an individual tribe or settlement is the culmination of some collaborative work, it is the beginning of another phase in the process as the students share their work and hear the testimonies of others. The combined reports and the exchanges between "legislators" and "experts" inform students further about the need for reparations and the possible forms for reparations.

THE HEARING

We have tried to stage the legislative hearing to appear as authentic as possible. In the school's library, a long table for the legislative committee faces a table for the panel of experts. A "gallery" allows room for students to observe and await their turn to testify before the committee. The committee members dress in business attire. The committee chair announces the commencement of proceedings and offers introductory remarks about the purpose of the hearing and the significance of such hearings as part of a legislative process. A "published" agenda projects the order of the proceedings, including the sequence of experts' testimonies.

The formality of the proceedings, along with the gravity of the conduct of the committee, adds to the sense of authenticity in the simulation and inspires students to "up their game" and take their parts seriously. While the presenters before the committee have the most significant role, we have also given the observers access to laptops and tablets to post comments and reactions on an established blog site. These blog postings become an evolving record of the proceedings as students are synthesizing the whole sequence of interactions and composing their reports and recommendations to the legislators. In schools without access to such technology, it would be useful to ask students to record reactions in journals or in informal "exit slips" that the teacher can compile for sharing across a class.

We offer below an example of the testimony from one team of "experts." Following this sample testimony is an example of a question-and-answer exchange between the team and the members of the committee.

> *Lucy:* We are representing the Mohawk tribe. We suffered many losses both in land and our cultural identity at the hands of the European settlers. Our ancestors occupied the land that is now known as New York. For as long as we remember our ancestors lived in this area. Family was and is very important to us. Family groups shared a long house and shared jobs, which allowed us to survive. Men were hunters, protectors, traders, and chiefs. The women took care of the family, farmed, cooked, and made the clothing. We were very protective and careful of the land in which we lived and we were forced off of it.

Bob: We had many very important traditions that defined our culture and we had a very organized way of living. Our spiritual beliefs were very important to us. We believed everything on earth had a spirit. We had many ceremonies and celebrations. Our government structure was groundbreaking. The men were the chiefs but only the women were allowed to elect the chiefs. There was a wartime chief and peacetime chief. Everyone in the council of chiefs had to be in agreement before any action could take place. Our government was so well organized that Benjamin Franklin used it as a model for the constitution for the 13 colonies.

Tom: Although the European explorers and settlers called us savages, tricked us into signing treaties in which our land was lost, destroyed our villages, food, and wealth, we still respected and tried to help the newcomers. As recently as the 1900s, White people were trying to destroy our culture by placing our children in boarding schools and isolating them from their family and culture.

Stella: For all this damage, we ask for the following:

- We require a sincere apology from the president of the United States of America.
- To gain respect for our culture, we want every level of school— elementary, middle, and high school—to teach an accurate lesson about the cultural life of American Indians.
- We deserve the return of some of our land. We survived on undeveloped land, meaning forests, plains, or land with lakes, rivers and streams. This is the type of land we want returned us.
- Each tribe should receive $5 million to rebuild their nation and make their community stronger.

"Senator" McCann: Thank you very much for your testimony here today. I can see that you have done some careful research to prepare for today's hearing. But I have a few questions, and I expect that the other members of the committee will have questions as well. First, you say that you want land returned to you. That land that was taken away generations ago is now occupied by other people who paid money for it. What will become of them?

Lucy: Well, they could pay them for their land and then give it back to the Mohawks.

McCann: So the government would figure out some appropriate price for each piece of land and then compensate the current occupant?

Lucy: That's right.

"Senator" Kahn: How will you guarantee that each school will be teaching accurate lessons about the Mohawks and other tribes?

Bob: You could check all the history books and make sure that they don't leave out important stuff about the way that the Native

Americans lived and how they had land and other stuff taken away from them.

"Senator" Galas: How did you decide that $5 million would be an appropriate amount for compensation?

Stella: We kind of estimated. We guessed that that would be an okay amount of money to at least start rebuilding things to try to get back to the way they were before their land was taken away.

These follow-up exchanges between the "legislators" and the students encouraged the students to think about some of the complications behind their policy recommendations and their reasoning for offering any course of action for reparations. The exchanges as well as the debriefing sessions that followed were designed to help the learners to develop an inner critical voice that suggested the questions that critics might raise and the expectations for reasoned judgments.

CLASSROOM DEBRIEFING

The testimony of each panel is powerful in itself, but the aggregation of all the testimonies equips students with a view of the breadth and significance of the harms experienced by various groups when Native Americans and non-Native settlers came into conflict. After the simulated hearing involving the combined classes, each class returned to its own classroom to make sense of what students had witnessed. Here is an example from Becky D'Angelo's class:

Ms. D'Angelo: Now that you have heard the reports from the various groups, what have you decided? Do you think the Native Americans have valid complaints? If so, what can we do now to repair harms done in the past?

Brett: They should give back land to the Cherokee because it seems that they have a very developed civilization. Plus they destroyed everything the Cherokee had.

Ava: So are you going to kick off the people who live on that land, Brett?

Bobby: They should get reparations because Jackson turned the U.S. agents against them [the Cherokee] even though the Cherokee saved his life. They should give back land.

Ms. D'Angelo: What about the people who currently live on this land?

Brett: I guess it is not that easy.

Rebecca: I agree with Ms. D'Angelo and Brett. It's not easy to get all the land back and the people that live there can't just become homeless. Maybe some land where they lived would be good.

Ava: They should get a meaningful SORRY because so many people died moving from one place to another. Four thousand people died on the Trail of Tears. That's so sad.

Brett: I think that they should get all of Montana.

Ms. D'Angelo: Montana has a lot of ranchers who would not want to give up their land. They have owned this land for generations and provide the country with food.

Rebecca: I agree with Brett. They were a very developed civilization and it's sad how the non-Natives took all their land. So maybe they should give them an apology and land if necessary. But I really do think people should apologize. Maybe people who have ancestors that came here could do it.

Evan: I agree with Ms. D'Angelo because you can't just move the people who live there.

Lauren: I think it's unfair that people took things from the Sioux like their sacred buffalo. People killed them and just left the dead animals lying on the ground with no help for the tribe and also took their food source [buffalo]. How would they get food when almost all of the buffaloes were gone?

Clark: I think they do have valid complaints because the White men treated the Sioux badly by killing the sacred buffalo and the government didn't back the Sioux up. Also, the Sioux children were sent to schools that taught White ways. Some reparations might be making reservation life better, giving the Sioux an apology, and make their life better in other ways.

Drew: Just give them some money so people that are American Indians have some money to live because money is power.

Rebecca: Money power? Really. It's not just money. You can't use money to bring people back alive. They stole the civilization. Money can't just repay [that].

Lauren: Do you think that the president of the U.S.A. should say a sincere apology? Shouldn't we have all of America say a sincere apology?

Ava: That might be too much work and not all of America caused harm to Native Americans.

Gracie: I agree that we should say sorry. I like the idea of a monument for the Native Americans.

Bobby: I think they should make monuments in Washington, DC, where everyone can see them. They deserve it.

While the students struggle with the logistical and legal details involved in any program of reparations, they recognize that grievous harms have been committed, and they invoke their earlier "rules" for reparations to judge where reparations are appropriate and what form they should take.

Students also recognize that, and sometimes express frustration because the solutions that they propose will have messy consequences in order to advance the cause of justice. This messiness is part of history, an element in inquiry, and part of determining policy in a just society. It is important that students understand the complications involved in finding solutions or just responses to difficult policy questions, even the difficulty of interpreting accurately what happened.

PROMPT FOR INDIVIDUAL WRITING: THE REQUEST FOR REPARATIONS

Story Review: Students are reminded of the congressional legislative committee's proposed action on a bill that would guarantee reparations for all members of their tribes. They understand that the principle behind the idea of reparations is that the central government of the United States, representing the whole nation, must take collective responsibility for the many harms experienced by Native Americans since the arrival of European settlers to the continent. Under this idea of reparations, the government is held responsible for not adequately protecting people from harm, and in some instances for initiating or perpetuating the harm. The advocates for the reparations bill point to the following harms as cause for reparations:

- deceptive and unfair treaties
- physical attacks on Native American communities
- deceptive trade practices
- enslavement
- the spread of deadly viral diseases
- the suppression of Native American culture to near-extinction
- the humiliating depiction of Native Americans as godless, ignorant savages

Some critics have been quick to point out the harms that Native Americans have caused to European settlers and their descendants. In some instances the critics have recommended that the Native American tribes compensate the descendants of European settlers. The committee has to take these claims into consideration.

The advocates for the reparations bill would like to see that a new law would guarantee certain compensations for the Native American tribes. They have suggested the following possibilities:

- a *universal apology* that candidly admits that the federal government over several generations has sponsored or tolerated harms to Native Americans

- monetary compensation for *each* tribe member of at least $10,000
- the return of all tribal lands to the current tribal councils to decide their distribution and future use, even if this means the displacement of current residents on those lands
- the banning of all Native American images and symbols for use as commercial logos and team mascots
- a comprehensive program of education in the public schools to inform students about the harms and injustices that European settlers have caused Native Americans for hundreds of years
- a program of public service messages to elevate the image and prestige of Native American cultures

Talking to Your Classmates: Talk to your classmates about these possibilities. *What do you think would be the best way for the federal government to respond to the requests for reparations?* For each action, explain why you think this is a fair or unfair compensation for the things that Native Americans claim that they have suffered for hundreds of years. Your judgments should rely on the guidelines your class developed for deciding reparations claims. You will want to take notes during the discussion so that you have notes ready for a written response.

Writing to the Chair of the Committee: Representative Philip Uster wants to know what, if anything, you think legislators *should* do to compensate Native American tribes and to make amends for harms to a whole group of people. *Write a letter to Representative Philip Uster to explain.* Your letter should include the following:

- *Describe briefly* the situation you are writing about.
- *Recommend the actions* that the Congress and the nation should take. *Explain why* you think each action is necessary and fair. Draw from your research and the research of classmates, and rely on your guidelines for reparations to make your case. *Refer to the collected information* from the testimonies and reports, and *explain the significance* of the information by connecting it to the "rules" for reparation.
- If you disagree with any of the demands that Native American tribes have made, explain why these steps would not be appropriate or fair. Again, *draw from your research* and the research of your classmates, and rely on the guidelines for reparations.
- At the end, *summarize* what you think of the requests for reparations, and what you think the members of Congress should do.

SUMMATIVE RESPONSE

A long sequence of discussion- and inquiry-based activities has positioned students to produce an elaborated response to a problem that often perplexes adults. The discussions about the concept of reparations allowed students to construct criteria for judging when reparations are necessary and the form they should take. The practice with a school-based situation allowed the students to practice the moves of argument as they applied their rules in thinking about the facts of the case. Students expanded their thinking by gathering and sharing research, responding to questions from skeptics, and debriefing about the implications of all they had heard and read, including the blog posts. Readers will see the transfer of the purposeful talk among peers and the effects of collaboration in the following representative example of students' letters of advice to the legislator considering sponsorship of a reparations bill.

Student Letter to Legislator

Dear Representative Uster:

I appreciate your interest in the history and current condition of Native Americans. When the settlers arrived in America, the first people they met were the Natives. At first the Natives and settlers got along but as Jamestown grew, fights broke out between them. In the end the Native Americans' land, culture, and children were taken. Now they are demanding reparation.

Native Americans are not like most non-Natives might think. They had certain religions with gods and myths. They built houses with high elements of architecture and had large family trees that go back farther than we can remember. All this was taken when the settlers came to America.

The first act of reparation they would like is a universal apology that candidly admits that the federal government, over several generations, has sponsored or tolerated the harms to Native Americans. I think this is a reasonable request especially since it's true. Congress is only now addressing it because the Native Americans brought it to court.

Next, they want a monetary compensation for each tribe member in the amount of at least $10,000. I think this is a selfish and unreasonable request. First of all, if the government had that much money, they wouldn't just be giving it away. There can be more than 50 people in only one tribe! Do you have any idea of how much that would be!? I think maybe $1,000 to each tribe would be much more reasonable so they could pay off their debts and re-buy land that is for sale.

A third request is the return of all tribal lands to the current tribal councils to decide the distribution and future use even if this means displacement of current residents on those lands. No way! That is not fair! For example, if a person from Germany came to Elmhurst, Illinois, and bought a house with their own money that they had earned and worked to get, they would have to move out because the Native Americans want their land back. It is not fair because this person had nothing to do with the problems between the settlers and the Natives. The Indians know how it feels to have land taken from them against their will. If they took land from us, they would just be starting a chain reaction. In a couple of hundred years, we would probably demand the land back from them.

Another request they came up with is the banning of all Native American images and symbols for use as commercial logos and team mascots. I agree. If the Natives had won the war, I am quite sure that we wouldn't use those symbols. Just because we won, we seem to think we can use their images even if we haven't asked. It is their image and it was wrong to take it.

Another suggested compensation was to start a comprehensive program of education in public schools to inform students about the harms and injustices that the European settlers have caused to Native Americans for hundreds of years. I don't think this is necessary for all schools. I say this because in our school we already learn about it. I do think schools that don't teach these things, should do so.

The last thing they want is a program of public service messages to elevate the image and prestige of Native American cultures. I think considering all the harms that we have done to them this is a reasonable request. We need to do this.

Considering this letter, I hope you will make a fair choice for the Natives.

Sincerely,
Ellie Tierney

This letter from a 5th-grader to a U.S. representative is not without its flaws, but a reader can see the positive effect of the many forums in which Ellie participated. Ellie's letter shows that she has learned a lot about Native American cultures and has grown to appreciate their civilizations and the harms that many tribes have suffered.

The letters to Representative Uster are one form of assessment to reveal the extent of the content and skills that the students have learned during their inquiry into the reparations problem. The students' written analyses depend on their accurate representation of events in history and the application of a reasonable standard to evaluate the significance and implications of those events. Through their active participation, students gain some appreciation of a process of government designed to solve problems and protect residents. Other learning outcomes, such as consistent listening to peers, encouraging participation, and advocating for inclusion in the team process, are more difficult to measure, but we have seen students from day to day engage with one another in rational and civil discourse to negotiate appropriate steps to take in contending with problems that often seem to be the reserve of the adult world. In short, we think that active participation in the kind of learning experiences that we report throughout this book prepares students for responsible citizenship and perhaps helps them to recognize that democracy is both a process and an attitude of what Dewey (2008) calls "associated living, a conjoint communicated experience" (p. 93), measuring individual action against the effect that it has on a whole community.

LEARNING FROM ACTIVE ENGAGEMENT

Over many years of teaching and of relying on simulations and other inquiry-based activities, we have heard a few colleagues note both obliquely and directly that we are engaging students in frivolous "play" while other teachers are directing learners in more serious endeavors. While we readily admit to engaging students in a kind of play, we contend that this play is anything but frivolous. We hope that students experience many of the same conditions that we all enjoy during play: being lost in the moment, totally invested in the endeavor, losing track of time and distractions—the kind of "flow" experience that Csikszentmihalyi (1990) describes. The exhilaration in interacting, sharing, and sometimes contending with peers was not the goal in itself but the means toward helping students learn social studies concepts and content and the important procedures for reading critically, synthesizing and evaluating information, and formulating complex arguments for a specific audience. The procedures included an array of literacy skills—reading flexibly and critically, listening attentively and critically, and writing logically and coherently. In designing a simulation role-playing activity, we were mindful of Common Core State Standards for literacy and other standards for disciplinary thinking in social studies, consistent with the C3 Framework. Figure 2.1 accounts for the complex of learning that students experience during the sequence of activities described in Chapters 1 and 2.

In addition to aligning with the key literacy goals listed above, the learning activities described throughout this book are consistent with the themes in the C3 Framework for Social Studies State Standards (NCSS, 2013). The inquiry-based activities help students to recognize essential questions associated with history, economics, and civics. Students learn processes of research

Figure 2.1. Literacy and Social Studies Learning During the Reparations Sequence

1. **Students learn substantial social studies content.**

   - Who were the Native American tribes/nations who lived in North America, especially in the Northeast and in the areas that came to be known as the Mid-Atlantic states in the United States?
   - How did these tribes live? What were defining elements in their cultures?
   - What were the initial and long-term experiences of the tribes in their encounters with European settlers to the region?
   - What were the experiences of European settlers as they founded communities in the lands that were once common to Native Americans?

2. **Students learn and apply procedures for research.**

   - Students find sources of information.
   - Students judge the relevance and accuracy of sources of information.
   - Students judge the reliability of sources of information.
   - Students select and synthesize various sources of information relevant to a research focus.
   - Students organize research notes to support subsequent oral and written reports.

Note: See Common Core Standard RI.5.7: Draw on information from multiple print or digital sources, demonstrating the ability to locate an answer to a question quickly or to solve a problem efficiently.

3. **Students read both fiction and nonfiction texts related to Native Americans and their encounters with European settlers.**

   - Students respond to their reading with written and oral comments.
   - Students link various readings to one another.
   - Students advance their reading fluency through the volume of texts they read.
   - Students expand their reading and writing vocabulary.
   - Students develop an enthusiasm for reading through their positive experience with a series of texts.

Note: See Common Core Standard RI.5.10: By the end of the year, read and comprehend informational texts, including history/social studies, science, and technical texts, at the high end of the Grades 4–5 text complexity band independently and proficiently.

4. **Students write elaborated arguments in response to a significant policy question.**

   - Students introduce a topic by framing a problem for their readers.
   - Students overtly express a position relative to a proposition of policy.
   - Students support general claims with relevant and accurate information, examples, or both.

Figure 2.1. Literacy and Social Studies Learning During the Reparations Sequence
(continued)

- Students interpret their support for claims.
- Students represent opposing views fairly and accurately.
- Students evaluate the merits of opposing positions.

Note: See Common Core Standard W.5.1: Write opinion pieces on topics or texts, supporting a point of view with reasons and information.

5. **Students present information and analysis in oral reports.**

- Students speak to an audience with the diction, volume, and pacing appropriate to the audience and context.
- Students present ideas in an organized and coherent form.
- Students listen attentively to questions and respond with relevant answers delivered in the tone appropriate for the audience and situation.

Note: See Common Core Standard SL.5.4: Report on a topic or text or present an opinion, sequencing ideas logically and using appropriate facts and relevant, descriptive details to support main ideas or themes; speak clearly at an understandable pace.

6. **Students deliberate about a significant policy question and work toward consensus.**

- Students listen actively to several speakers.
- Students take notes on the contributions of several speakers.
- Students represent and evaluate the positions of several speakers.
- Students contribute their judgments toward resolving a policy question.
- Students identify common ground among competing speakers.

Note: See Common Core Standard SL.5.1: Engage effectively in a range of collaborative discussions (one-on-one, in groups, and teacher-led) with diverse partners on *grade 5 topics and texts*, building on others' ideas and expressing their own clearly.

7. **Students work collaboratively with members of a research team.**

- Students identify the goals of a team project.
- Students divide the components of a complex task.
- Students contribute their efforts toward completing a complex task.
- Students use appropriate conflict resolution strategies as necessary, for example, paraphrasing, withholding judgments, and finding common understanding.

Note: See Common Core Standard SL.5.1: Engage effectively in a range of collaborative discussions (one-on-one, in groups, and teacher-led) with diverse partners on *grade 5 topics and texts*, building on others' ideas and expressing their own clearly.

as they tackle the questions raised in class and have opportunities to apply the procedures during subsequent occasions. The research processes include students' gaining access to both print and online sources of information and judging their relevance and validity. Learners engage with one another in grappling with problems, communicate results of their research and deliberations, and argue for specific policies.

In the following chapters we offer similar learning activities. The chapters offer two more extended simulation "games," with each having a different format. The examples focus on different eras of American history, and certainly do not exhaust possibilities for periods of history and problems essential to social studies.

CHAPTER 3

Living the Colonial Experience

When 5th-grade student Tyler entered the classroom on a Monday morning, he brought with him the oversized political cartoon that he had drawn on poster board over the weekend. His drawing (Figure 3.1) depicted a heartless puppet master king extracting money from the pocket of a helpless colonist. Annie arrived with a model of what she imagined her family's Colonial silver shop to be, with carefully fitted Popsicle sticks shaping the floor and walls, and foam core board cutouts making the shelves, displays, and counter (Figure 3.2). Other students brought in homemade maps of the town and region, floor plans for their Colonial homes, and pamphlets to protest against the king and Parliament. In other classes these artifacts might have been the assigned projects to reveal what students had learned during a unit of instruction; in this case, the students had completed the projects on their own, with no solicitation from the teacher. Apparently the learners were engrossed enough in their lived experience as pre–Revolutionary War colonists to give expression in various ways to what they were experiencing, feeling, and thinking, including through the more formal writing that appears later in this chapter.

As students entered the classroom and checked the agenda on the board, they were pleased to see an item that read "Elmtown Meeting," which meant that this was a day when they would pretend to be colonists at a town hall meeting, tackling the problems of the period, issues including political events that caused upheavals in the homes of many of the town residents, as well as the various risks of disease, sick livestock, bad weather, crime, and accidents. Instead of relying on only the streamlined narratives written by others in a history book, they would immerse themselves in the period by living in a colonist role.

On this Monday, the students had already discussed in their "families" how the Quartering Act would affect their families and their businesses. As we explain later in this chapter, the teacher organized students into "family" groups of three or four, giving them a general identity—small farmer, shopkeeper, fisherman, innkeeper. When a teacher called the town hall meeting to order, a member of each family joined the problem-solving process at the meeting table. A volunteer from one family introduced the topic of the day.

Figure 3.1. Tyler's Political Cartoon

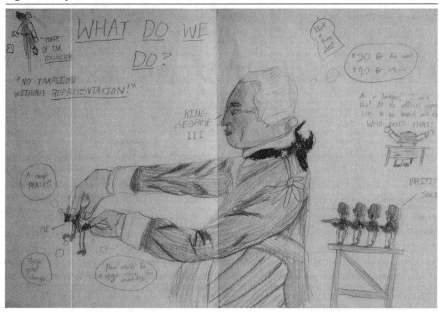

Figure 3.2. Annie's Depiction of the Silversmith's Shop

Tyler: So, the thing that happened, the new thing from the king, is that we are supposed to let soldiers live with us. We have to give them a place to sleep and feed them.

Mr. McCann: Okay, this is what I understand to be the Quartering Act, that we are supposed to provide "quarters," or room and board, for the British soldiers in our community.

Tyler: Yeah. So we have to pay extra to keep these soldiers.

Burton: And I don't know why the soldiers are here.

Mr. McCann: First I want to hear how this new act has affected Mr. Ridgeway's family. Mr. Ridgeway [i.e., Tyler], how has this Quartering Act affected your family and what do you propose we should do about it?

Tyler: We are large landowners, so keeping a soldier or two won't be a big deal. But for some family like the Curtises, they would have to pay extra to have someone else in their house. It would be like having another family member that they have to give food to.

Mr. McCann: Mr. Thistle.

Burton: Yeah. We are poor fishermen and we don't have a lot of money to be feeding soldiers.

Lexi: Out of order.

Mr. McCann: What do you mean?

Lexi: Burton, I mean Mr. Thistle, is suppose to summarize what Mr. . . . Mr. Ridgeway said first.

Burton: Uh . . . uh. Tyler, I mean Mr. Ridgeway, said that we will have to let soldiers stay in our homes and we have to feed them. He wouldn't have it so bad, but he is worried about other people.

Mr. McCann: Is that right, Mr. Ridgeway?

Tyler: Yes. That's it.

Mr. McCann: Mr. Thistle, do you want to continue?

Burton: We make just enough money to feed ourselves, and we don't want to have to feed a soldier and let him sleep at our house. We wouldn't know the soldiers, would we?

Mr. McCann: Miss Curtis, or is it Mrs. Curtis?

Lexi: Miss. Well, he said that his family would suffer from having to feed the soldiers and keep them in their house. And we don't know who these soldiers are. We got this letter from a cousin in England. She said that the soldiers aren't always the, you know, the best citizens.

Mr. McCann: You mean *subjects*, don't you?

Lexi: Yeah, the best subjects. I mean, sometimes the poorest people join the army because they can't do anything else. And some of the soldiers came out of prisons. So these people would be in our homes. It would be creepy to have a stranger living with you. And you don't even know if they are criminals or something.

Mr. McCann: Let me get this straight. I have heard different reports about this act. I have heard that the community has to take the responsibility for the care of the soldiers, but you don't actually have to take them into your home. I have also heard reports that you would be forced to house and feed some soldiers in your own homes. So which is it? Mrs. Palmer.

Trish: We got a letter from someone in New York who said that they had to let a soldier stay in their own house. I don't like that. We have young children in our family and we want them to be safe. And it costs more to pay for the soldiers.

Burton: I agree with Mrs. Palmer. We already pay more taxes for sugar and molasses and other stuff. Now it will cost more to pay for the soldiers. I think we should build a separate place, like a barn, to let the soldiers stay away from our families.

Mr. McCann: I don't understand, Mr. Thistle. These are the soldiers from your homeland. I would think you would want to show respect for these soldiers who have been sent here to protect us.

Tyler: Yeah, but we don't need their protection. I agree with Mrs. Palmer and Mr. Thistle. The war is over and we are not allowed to move west into Indian territory, so what are they protecting us against? Maybe we should tell the king that we don't need protection and don't need the soldiers.

In this brief exchange, the students seem well under way to experiencing in some small degree what colonists must have felt like when they faced the prospect of quartering strangers in their own homes and judging the appropriateness of taking care of the king's military personnel. The U.S. history textbooks that we have seen over the years present a seamless narrative that emphasizes the inevitability of the independence of the united colonies in North America; the foresight, wisdom, courage, rectitude, and determination of the revolutionaries among the colonies; and the united effort to throw off the shackles of monarchy. As Moreau (2004) and Zimmerman (2002) demonstrate, market demands and pressures from various interest groups have influenced textbook producers to publish textbooks that depict U.S. history in the least controversial way, which only leads to more controversy about the sidestepping of conflicts. We have found students disengaged with their textbook reading and argue that the textbooks have failed to serve students in helping them to understand deeply how events would unite people across several distinct regions and provoke them to risk their lives, their fortunes, and their "sacred Honor" to advance the "glorious cause" of independence. We wanted to see students draw from their extensive speaking with one another and from their readings to explain to others how a complex of historical, cultural, economic, and political events and conditions moved Colonial leaders and thousands of ordinary people to risk everything to secure independence and embark on a prolonged experiment in self-governance. In short, we wanted to see that in their writing, students could trace and explain the causes that led to the effect that we know as the American Revolution.

What we did not anticipate was that when students imagined themselves as late 18th-century colonists, they would engage in conversations that echo contemporary debates about the role of a central government, the extent of individual freedoms, and the recourse of citizens to oppose government. We have seen such conversations occurring again and again among our students, in civil forums that rely more on the power of reason than on vehemence, histrionics, and personal rancor to persuade others of the value of policy and of the call to action. At the same time, we can well imagine that a teacher who invites students in American public schools to question popular accounts of the "Boston Massacre" or to view critically some of the pantheon of American leaders could endure some heat from members of the community who prefer the study of U.S. history as a celebration rather than a disciplined inquiry and critical appraisal. As Zimmerman (2002) points out, much of the cultural wars related to U.S. history textbooks have been about *who* is included in the representation of history; but another source of contention has to do with whether or not we consider competing views about events and their significance (p. 214).

The following chapter offers a simulation of living in a Colonial town in the years preceding the Revolutionary War and the Declaration of Independence. The simulation is essentially a series of town hall meetings that immerse students in team problem solving and deliberation about significant political events. The purposeful talk extends into reading of primary source and constructed texts, which we provide as appendixes. We have witnessed over several years that the talking, listening, and readings position students to write elaborated responses to, and reflections about, the experiences that they have "lived." The purpose of this chapter is to suggest ways to prepare students for their purposeful work together and to show how the simulation looks in action.

THE SIMULATION AT A GLANCE

As we note in our Introduction and illustrate in Chapters 1 and 2, the simulation will have a few key features that invite students into a process of inquiry that involves reading, writing, and a lot of talk. For Colonial Elmtown, here are the important elements:

- *The Constructed Environment:* Students enter into the world of pre–Revolutionary War Massachusetts, with special attention to the constraints on communication, commerce, and travel.

- *New Identities:* The students form six families and construct new identities within prescribed parameters.
- *Problems:* The overarching problem concerns the responses to an increasingly oppressive king and Parliament, and then there are the daily problems of failed crops, sick livestock, accidents, bad weather, and so on.
- *Information:* Through the documents that the teacher provides and the research that students do on their own, there is sufficient information to support the thinking about the series of political and economic crises.
- *Pathway:* The series of stages, each building on the preceding one, lead down a path to the most crucial decision—whether or not to declare and fight for independence.
- *Forums:* Each family discusses how various events affect the members of the family and threaten their hopes and contentment. A representative from each family joins in the town hall meeting at each stage to deliberate and decide how the community should respond to the objectionable actions.
- *Synthesis and Reflection:* At each stage, each Elmtown resident writes in a journal about the current events, and a team of writers composes a "consensus report" for the community. At the end of the series of stages, each resident writes a summary report, which could be a narrative, an explanation, or an appeal.

PREPARING TO ENTER A DIFFERENT ENVIRONMENT

When students (or video game players) enter into any simulated environment, they need to understand the rules and constraints of that environment. For living in Colonial Elmtown, students will need to appreciate two concepts that are distinctly different from their modern world. First, as their parents have probably often stressed, they need to appreciate the value of money. Of course, currency in Colonial North America was far from stable, with coins of many realms being exchanged, but students should have an idea of how an English pound might translate into a modern dollar. In addition, the participants need to recognize the distinction in value between an 18th-century pound and a modern pound. And then how do you convert this projection into modern dollars?

The second constraint concerns concepts of distance, time, travel, and communication. If a local resident dares to participate in a Stamp Act Congress in Philadelphia, what would be the distance, and how much time would it take to travel that distance? In addition, if the king wants to be current about the events in his colonies, how long would it take to get word to him? Or, how long would it take troops to travel to North America to suppress an insurrection?

Gaining an appreciation of these two issues—money and distance—provides an opportunity for applied mathematics for those students who wish to inquire further. Of course, there is no definitive way to calculate the modern equivalent for any amount of money from the late 18th century, but several online sources suggest ways to think about the problem. Some students will enjoy taking on the challenge of converting values from the late 18th century to their modern equivalent. Table 3.1 invites some simple algebraic thinking to insert values in the blank cells and complete the chart. Of course, the conversion from item to item is not exact, because items such as sugar would have been more scarce and therefore more expensive during Colonial times. The few students who want to tackle the calculation and further research can share with others in order to allow all students to appreciate how a succession of taxes might impinge on a family's happiness and sense of independence. In our experience, the contributions from these volunteers have informed a sense of the economic impact of the various measures of the king and Parliament. In a small way, this obligation to understand the reality of the historic moment replicates some of what historians do when they read the events of history as the players in history would have experienced them rather than from the presumptions of today.

Table 3.1. Calculating Roughly Equivalent Values

Item	1774 dollars	21st-century dollars
1 pound (currency)	2.40	67.00
1 loaf of bread		1.00
1 lb. sugar		
a book		
a musket		
a mule		
a horse		
1 bushel of salt		18.00
1 lb. tea		4.50
1 lb. wheat flour		2.50
teacher's annual salary	144.00	4,020.00

PREVIEWING THE LANGUAGE OF THE SIMULATION

As students participate in the Colonial Elmtown experience, they will need to be familiar with some of the vocabulary embedded in the descriptions of the families and the events that affect them. They will also need to know some special academic vocabulary associated with the directions. In other words, students will need to know what they will be expected to do, sometimes referred to as the "primary language function." Our experience with students in upper elementary school, middle school, and early high school tells us that many students will benefit from a preview of the following words and expressions:

> **Content Language:** boycott, compromise, consensus, contentious, facilitator, imperiled, inflammatory, intolerable, intrusion, mediation, merchant class, proclamation, protocol, provocative, tranquility, unanimous, unfettered, unification, unimpeded, upheaval.

> **Academic Language:** recommend a course of action, summarize, support a claim or recommendation, explain the significance of evidence, summary report, consensus report, write an appeal.

As we suggest in Chapter 2, there are many possibilities for introducing students to vocabulary that will help them with their reading and writing. One thing we know for sure: Students won't get much out of writing down a dictionary definition and using selected words in their own constructed sentences. We suggest that over the days preceding the simulation, the teacher work some of the words into the everyday discourse of the classroom. Without much difficulty, a teacher can infuse daily conversations with words like *consensus, contentious, intolerable, tranquility, unfettered,* and *unimpeded.*

Many teachers have a variety of such approaches to introducing key content vocabulary. It is especially important that a teacher also introduce the academic vocabulary attached to directions and expectations. For English language learners, this is crucial. If a teacher wants students to *frame* problems, *summarize* contributions, *support* claims, *interpret* evidence, and *synthesize* arguments, then she will want to demonstrate these processes explicitly and label them overtly.

As we explain in Chapter 1, a teacher will also need to foreground any complicated simulation and problem solving with some rudimentary work in civil discourse and argument. Students will benefit from contributing to an expression of the standards for instructional conversations and from having many opportunities to interact with one another in a purposeful way.

FACILITATING EXTENSIVE TALK

In order for the town hall meetings to function productively and lead to a consensus about action, we provided a framework to help the participants converse in a civil and responsible way. We established as a convention that each town hall meeting began with a volunteer reporting what current event had occurred in Elmtown. This speaker then described the event's impact on the family and community and recommended a course of action (a petition, a boycott, a letter, etc.). Any subsequent speaker would paraphrase the previous speaker, check for the accuracy of this representation, agree or disagree, and then offer his or her own analysis and family's perspective. Sometimes the teacher/facilitator summarized the line of commentary across several speakers, or called on a student to provide the summary, which amounted to a synthesis of several reports and recommendations. The teacher/facilitator also asked questions to clarify and prompt students to offer specific support for their recommendations. For example, we recall a student suggesting that a possible response to the Quartering Act could be for the residents of Elmtown to lock their doors and pretend to be away from home. If other students didn't question this suggestion, the teacher/facilitator might say, "Let me get this straight: You plan to resist the most powerful military in the world by locking your door? And how long would you have to maintain this attempt at fooling the soldiers?"

Skills at facilitating discussions and at participating in discussion develop with practice. We suggest that the dialogic moves essential to the game should not be novel when the students enter the world of Elmtown but should be practiced elements in the daily discourse of the classroom (McCann, 2014; McCann, Johannessen, Kahn, & Flanagan, 2006). We recognize that the talk among the students during their "family" discussions and during the town hall meetings allows the learners to practice the procedures that become important for their writing and for their critical analysis of texts. But we do not want to presume anything. As facilitators of the discussions we listen for and encourage the kind of oral expression that students can transform into their written texts: summarizing the current events, evaluating the event's impact on family and community, citing the assessment of impact in supporting a recommendation for action, referring to other speakers and respectfully evaluating their contributions, and citing letters and other texts as evidence to show that reports are accurate and that claims and recommendations are warranted. These elements of deliberation are part of the "game" and serve as the rules by which families earn credit. A rubric for evaluating speaking and listening appears in Appendix B.

With attention to the purpose for each discussion forum, the teacher/facilitator can listen for the elements to promote during the discourse. Sometimes it is necessary to slow the process to remind the students about the rules of the game and to model the kind of talk that deliberation and respectful debate require. Preceding the simulation, students should demonstrate the same speaking and listening proficiencies that the game requires. We recommend also that the teacher label and highlight the moves of discourse during daily responses to students: "Thank you for *summarizing* those events." "That was a good *synthesis* of what people have said here today." "I appreciate that you *connected* your contribution to what Georgina already said." "That sounds like *reasonable support* for what you recommend." In some ways, this flips the process: Instead of hearing about summarizing, synthesizing, evaluating, or supporting as abstract skills, the students practice these procedures in a meaningful context. The teacher can then help them to label what they have done and invite learners to reflect on how they accomplished these efforts.

As we note in Chapter 1, facilitating discussions is a *skill*. In order to sustain purposeful discussion, a teacher needs to keep in mind the function of the current discussion and the habits of thinking that she wants to cultivate. Sometimes the teacher has to prompt students to provide support for their recommendations, to interpret information, and to link their contributions to the contributions of others.

MOVING INTO A VARIETY OF TEXTS

Before we begin the Colonial Elmtown project, through our work with several texts we introduce students to the idea of colonization and Colonial life, especially by reading and discussing both fiction and nonfiction. We have found that students are curious to read more about the occupation represented by their Colonial family and about Colonial life in general. We judge that the earlier reparations unit, the reading about early Colonial life, and the reading related to Colonial Elmtown connect with the National Council for Social Studies standards about time continuity and change, helping students to appreciate how different groups at different times in our nation's history experienced and represented events and to recognize how a sequence of events resulted in lingering effects.

Some of the texts are primary source materials and constructed texts that we provide to help the students understand the details of the events, the impact on colonists, and the reactions on both sides of the ocean. Another function of our constructed letters and the primary source texts is that we are able to introduce the principal players in the rebellion, such as Thomas Paine, John Adams, Abigail Adams, Samuel Adams, John Dickinson, and Thomas Jefferson. We offer examples of our constructed letters in Appendix E.

We also enrich the simulated experience by introducing students to relevant historical fiction. We have found the following texts worthwhile for shared or independent reading, enriching students' understanding of the condition of the colonists and the real experience of war. Students might read these texts concurrently with the simulation game or as an extension of their Colonial experience. The titles below are just a few of the many possibilities, and we have listed others in Appendix K.

Chains by Laurie Halse Anderson addresses the price of freedom for both a nation and an individual. Set in New York during the days leading up to the American Revolution, the narrative brings to life the struggles of both the loyalists and the patriots without glorifying the patriot cause. The main character, Isabel, tells the story of her life as a slave in New York. Readers might be surprised to learn the extent to which slavery existed in both the middle and New England colonies. The well-researched novel provides answers to questions that readers may have about the time period it depicts.

Peter and Connie Roop (1986) offer an account of a Quaker boy and his family who become spies during the American Revolution in the short historical fiction *Buttons for General Washington*. It's a good way to introduce students to historical fiction in an easy-to-read format. Some of our less proficient readers enjoyed this book, which inspired an investigation into spies and spying during the Revolutionary era and a clandestine in-class formation of a spy ring to detect the loyalists among the townspeople.

Two other novels reveal the gruesome realities of the war. Many teachers will already be familiar with James and Christopher Collier's *My Brother Sam Is Dead* (1974) and Avi's *The Fighting Ground* (1984). Although the simulation focuses on the events that led to war, rather than the war itself, students often want to read more to learn about the events that followed from the years of provocation.

TRANSITIONING INTO WRITTEN REFLECTIONS

Our experience tells us that if students have been participating in discussions and keeping a daily journal of reports and reflections, they have much content to share when they are prompted to write a longer and more formal composition. They are ready to *narrate* the succession of events, *explain* how the events cause a strong response, *describe* how town hall meetings work and *evaluate* their effect, or *persuade* a leader about the need to change policy. In addition, with each stage at least one team of students collaborates on a "consensus report," sometimes requiring them to draw from postings on a blog site. These consensus reports (a letter to Parliament, a petition to the king, a pamphlet to stir up sentiment) provide an early rehearsal and important sources for the more complicated summative reports. Chapter 4 includes the prompts that offer students options for a written summation of their experience in Colonial Elmtown. In Appendix C we provide a rubric for assessing students' summative writing and offering them focused feedback. We suggest also that a teacher will want to respond regularly to journal entries and to the sequence of consensus reports.

But highly elaborated and coherent compositions do not automatically follow the extensive talk about problems and political crises. We guide students through a structured process that begins with a close examination of the writing prompts, including the glosses for key vocabulary, paraphrases of the task, and discussion of the choices. We also discuss students' expectations for the traits that would distinguish high-quality writing of this sort, leading to a review of the standard suggested by the rubric (Appendix C). As the students make their plans, drawing from their journals, the blog posts, and the consensus reports, they discuss with one another what they intend to write and how they intend to write it. Students then share drafts with classmates and the teacher, with feedback that draws from the language of the rubric.

We have found that many students prefer to write a narrative about the experience. They write to an imagined friend or relative in England or in another colony. Many of these compositions are too long to share here, with some efforts taking the form and length of a novella. Some students, provoked as they are by the loss of liberty and the imposition of increasingly onerous taxes, prefer to address an appeal directly to the king to change his treatment of his subject in the colonies. Here is one example:

Sample Student Response

Your Highness King George III,
    I have owned and operated a small shop in Elmtown, Massachusetts for the past 20 years. I have supplied the people of Elmtown with food, supplies, luxury items, and even livestock. These last few years have caused me great harm. Because of your actions I have lost money, my shop is not doing well, my family is suffering. I have always been loyal to you and England, but am starting to change my mind. Your actions over the past 20 years have taken away our rights as British citizens. We do not have a say in Parliament. We are paying more for all items like paper, sugar, molasses, and glass. You have closed our harbors which has also impacted our trade and as a result our livelihood. You made us quarter the soldiers, and after the French and Indian War you said we could no longer move west. I do not want to go to War with England. War is a very bad thing. It will result in towns being burned to dust. People will be fighting everywhere. Deaths will occur on both sides, families will suffer. I call on you to send a representative to the colonies to help solve these problems. I do not want violence or to separate from my home country.

The following is a list of grievances that my fellow colonists and I feel are the most serious. Each one has taken away a right that we should have as a subject of England.

- The sugar act placed taxes on us without any input from us. This included taxes on sugar, molasses, and other luxury items. These taxes affected Mr. Eldridge, Elmtown's innkeeper, and myself the town shopkeeper. We had to pay too high prices for the goods we brought in and then we were forced to raise our prices. It is not right to tax without representation.
- Mr. Eldridge was again impacted by the Quartering Act. He was forced to house British soldiers in his inn for free and was forced to provide them with food. This kept him from earning money from paying customers. In addition, the quartering act affected all members of the town. Even people in small homes who themselves weren't getting enough food were forced to share with the soldiers. Here in Elmtown we agreed to provide housing in our commons.
- The Boston Tea Party resulted in the closing of the harbor. I couldn't get the shipments I needed for my store. Other town members couldn't send things out. You are destroying our livelihood.
- The Boston Massacre that took place in Boston has devastated the people of Elmtown. We the people of Elmtown have tried to keep the talk of war down. With this massacre of Boston citizens by the British Army is causing us to rethink who we support. We have called for the trial of those soldiers who fired and killed innocent men.

I call on you, King George, to send representatives to the colonies to discuss these problems and avoid War. We have sent letters and pamphlets numbering more than five. You must pay attention. The colonists are demanding the end to unfair taxes and the right to meet peacefully to decide the things that concern us. You cannot make decisions for people thousands of miles away. We want a say in Parliament, troops moved out, and taxes to be repealed. Only you can change things and avoid War.

Respectfully,
Jedadiah Smith (Alex)

In writing to King George III, Alex (aka Jedadiah Smith) responds to the writing prompt by

- staying true to her established identity
- describing the difficulties that she and her family have faced as a result of the king's decrees and the actions of Parliament
- addressing the king with appropriately deferential language

Several other features of Alex's writing resulted from, or were enhanced by, her participation in the frequent and extensive discussions over eight stages of the simulation. She supports his general proposition—that the king should send a representative to negotiate changes in policy—by detailing the harms suffered by Alex's family and other residents of Elmtown, noting the heavy burden of taxes, the imposition of the Quartering Act, the Boston Massacre, and the closing of Boston Harbor. She cites the plight of another resident, Mr. Eldridge (a classmate assuming this identity), who had testified in town hall meetings about the impact that the king's actions had on the management of his inn.

Alex's general strategy for persuasion seems to be citing these harms and appealing to the king to have some sympathy for the suffering of his subjects. The discussion of these harms and their impact were the focus of the series of town hall conversations. Not only does Alex cite the harms caused by specific taxes; she also interprets their significance by offering the general warrant that "it is not right to tax without representation." In constructing her argument, Alex cites specific "texts," which include the printed documents such as the letters and pamphlets (see Appendix E), families' "consensus reports," and the testimonies of her fellow colonists at the town hall meetings. While the oral testimonies are not *texts* in the traditional sense, as evidence and public records of harms to local residents, they serve the same function as printed material to illustrate and support general claims.

Alex also makes the rhetorical move of noting that the residents have long been loyal subjects and wish to remain so and to avoid military conflict. It is hard to attribute this rhetorical strategy to a specific classroom experience, but perhaps the decorum of the town hall meetings suggests a way to establish a connection with an audience and appeal to sympathy. Alex also notes that the residents have been patient, having already sent many appeals, "numbering more than five." Even Alex's syntax here may be the product of having read 18th-century documents and having assumed the identity of a colonist, which is all part of the fun.

On the whole, by Common Core standards for written expression, especially for argument, or by comparison with the writing of similar learners, Alex's writing seems to be quite exceptional for a 5th-grader. We judge that several factors affected the quality of Alex's written product, among them the writing prompt, the reference to sample texts, and the standard set by the rubric. But we see that she was helped mostly by the daily discourse that equipped her with a lot of information and allowed her practice in expressing arguments and in summarizing and evaluating the arguments of other speakers.

EXTENDING THE COLONIAL EXPERIENCE

Students have several opportunities to extend their Colonial experience. As we describe at the beginning of the chapter, students in our classrooms have produced many unsolicited artifacts—political cartoons, posters, maps, models, and newspapers. We suggest that these efforts be encouraged and celebrated as enrichments of the experience and not become assigned tasks. We know also that students have pursued their own research—about reports of King George's mental illness, about what really happened at the Boston "massacre," about treating illness, about military might and tactics, and so on. Students have also enthusiastically pursued both fiction and nonfiction reading about the period.

We see opportunities for schools to partner with a local college or university in a forum at which students from the school and the college and the teachers and professor examine the events in history and the enduring questions that they raise. We can see that such a forum could offer panel presentations and open discussions about compelling historical and contemporary questions: What led to the independence of the colonies? To what extent were the Colonial leaders justified in excluding women and protecting slavery in their vision of a new democratic nation? To what extent are individual colonies (or states today) independent, and to what extent are they bound by a central government? Such a forum or related conversations in the classroom could invite students to connect the issues that John Adams, Thomas Jefferson, Abraham Lincoln, William Seward, and others grappled with and the issues that still roil politicians and voters today when protection of local control and the securing of rights on one side looks like the suppression of civil liberties on another side. We are encouraged when students make such connections to their contemporary world by way of analogy to understand what troubled people long ago.

While students' formal summative writing about their experience as Colonial characters serves as a culmination of the activity, we also wanted to place the learners in the position of being historians. We understand that the work of some historians involves the close examination of competing accounts of events in order to offer a more accurate and synthesized view of matters. We ask all students to think like historians in evaluating the merits of two contrasting reports of events in order to recommend a more accurate accounting of events and their effect. When we invite students to "be a history sleuth," we ask them to consult with one another about two constructed accounts of the series of events that the students had been discussing. We provide the complex prompt for this activity in Appendix F. We offer an example of one student's written response, providing an analysis of competing views of events. Georgina's analysis is quite long, and we reproduce approximately two-thirds of it here.

Colonist vs. British
Viewpoint

By Georgina Tierney

The colonists are rebellious scum. King George is a greedy tyrant. This argument has been going on for far too long. Neither side has given in. Both are equally stubborn in the godliness of their cause. Amazingly different views upon the same events. And now the prospect of war darkens our horizon. We must dispel this approaching storm before it dumps it's unholy contents upon us.

Taxes

The whole affair started after the French & Indian War. While England had triumphed over her opponents, the effort had left the Crown in horrible debt. King George III believed that because the war had been fought on American soil, the Colonists should shoulder the fee of the war. The Colonists protested bitterly, saying that it was *England's* war, so England should help them fill the royal treasury. The English Parliament turned a deaf ear to the Colonists' complaints. Taxes were thus lain upon the Colonies; along with a proclamation. No subject of King George III may move West. For the King feared that if his subjects continued moving westward, the Indians would attack, seeing it as a threat to their hunting grounds. The King would then have to protect his subjects. Thus, another war would begin. Looking at the treasury after the Seven Year War, the King was not overly anxious to call his troops to battle quite so soon. While his subjects "across the pond" weren't exactly thrilled about this new order, they obeyed it. As events came to pass, taxes were added to the Colonies. Sugar Act, Stamp Act, Quartering Act, Townshend Act, – with each additional reason to empty pockets, the Colonists gradually came to suffer. For the Colonists were wealthy in land, not coins. And soil, however rich it may be, cannot feed hungry children. The British believe that the King & Parliament have every right to impose taxes upon the Colonies. The general Colonist population, to put it simply, didn't. But balance isn't black and white, good and evil, right and wrong, innocent and guilty. Balance is more of a gray on both sides. Compromise is key. I propose that Parliament reduces taxes upon the Colonies, and deal them out to the rest of the English population. Then the Colonists can stop complaining about the unfairness of it all. It isn't *nearly* as bad as they make it out to be. That would sort out the taxation problem, and help disperse the storm. But the storm isn't made of one single cloud, just as this argument isn't made from a single issue. Let us sort out this next problem, shall we?

Troops

British presence in the Colonies. This issue is closely related to taxes, seeing as the Quartering Act was the base of the problem. King George, after the French & Indian War, came to the conclusion that the savages from the West *were* savage, and that he had a whole 13 Colonies in danger from the wrath of the defeated Indians. Parliament agreed with the King; the Colonists needed the protection of the Royal Army. However, there was a problem. Because the Seven Year War had left the Crown in such debt, they did not have the funding to support the Army in the Colonies, so far away from home. There was the cost of transport across the sea, weaponry, clothing, food, shelter – Parliament simply did not have the money. But the Colonist could not be left unprotected! Yes, most households had a gun, and a man to handle it, but this was hardly equal to the English Military. Would that be a strong enough force to hold off the hostile natives? Parliament strongly doubted it. Then, it occurred to a member of the Parliament that because the Colonists were the ones being protected, then they should provide the essentials. What if they simply stationed a soldier or two at every household, and the residence of the home could provide their guests with food and shelter. If this was not possible, the community could find (or build) suitable barracks for the soldiers. Everyone was very enthusiastic with this idea, and without further ado they began to devise the Quartering Act. The Colonists, on the other hand, were not nearly as enthusiastic about the new order as their cousins.

There was error to the marvelous plan Parliament had decided to act upon, and that was the morale of the army itself. For if a man was found guilty of a crime, he is given two options. One is to serve their time in prison. Another is to serve in His Majesty's Army for as long as the judge was to sentence them to prison. Thus, most of the foot soldiers were criminals. While the brute force and little mercy was an upside in the Army, these rogues were not fitted entirely for house life. Many of the homes the soldiers were to be stationed in were those of families with young children. Parents and townspeople alike were worried about the safety of their children and possessions should criminals be let into the town, armed with guns. The worries were carried through the Colonies, inspiring fear and distrust towards the army upon their arrival. However, the Army's hostile welcome was not due only to worries about the safety of the offspring. As most

Colonists saw it, this was an indirect tax, meaning it wasn't known as a tax. A tax, by definition, is a law that requires certain groups of people to pay a fee on certain items. The Colonists were well within their rights about this. Soldiers should *not* have the right to demand room & board from residence. But the Quartering Act went unopposed, and sowed the seeds to the British occupation in Boston.

After the Boston Tea Party—an event in Boston with some Colonists called the "Sons of Liberty"—protesting against a tax on tea, called the Townshend Act, stole aboard an English ship disguised as Indians, and proceeded to dump the shipment of tea overboard. The King and his Parliament were horrified. The tea itself was worth hundreds of pounds, but the actions of the Sons of Liberty, why, it was treason! As punishment to the general population of Boston, Parliament closed Boston Port. The Englishmen back home were not happy with this proclamation. Innocent merchants, shipbuilders, sailors, and colonists would all suffer without the port to provide them with income from the goods they export, the import of things they could not independently produce, the jobs the port provided; many things that were essential to the life they led were stolen away from them through no fault of their own. Simply because some of their number had made a rather rash and unwise move, the whole city was to be punished? The poor colonists were outraged. They were willing to accept consequence for their actions, such as getting a burn from touching fire. But the Colonists felt rather as if they had gotten a burn simply for sitting by the fire. This was, obviously, distinctly unfair, and most Bostonians found themselves beginning to take a personal dislike to the Crown. Many joined the ever-growing Sons of Liberty to rebel against the "meddling Brits". The Parliament wasn't pleased with the effect they would have on the innocent, but they saw no other option. Boston needed to know that if they protested against the Crown's rule, the Crown would come back, twice as hard as they had before. In hindsight, this was not very logical in trying to get the loyalty and obedience of the Colonists. It's somewhat like saying, if the children don't love us, we will punish them until they do. But if you punish a person, or a whole group of persons for what they can see no fault in, they will not instantly part from their ways. If anything, they will only cling to them tighter.

THE EFFECT OF LITERACY AND HISTORY IN ACTION

The compositions by Alex and Georgina in this chapter are two of the more developed examples of writings from our classes, but all students completed quite elaborate writing and showed growth over the course of a semester. In their writing, the students demonstrated mature command of the events that would account for the formation of a new nation, and they revealed that they could think critically about the texts that they examined independently and discussed collaboratively. They drew from fiction, such as *My Brother Sam Is Dead* and *Fighting Ground*, and nonfiction texts, such as the selected primary source texts, to have something of substance to say in their compositions. They followed a structured process to prepare, draft, review, and revise their work. Perhaps most important, they "lived" the experience as colonists, which meant that they *felt* in some small degree how a military presence, restrictions on land acquisition, and the increasing of taxes and duties by a parliament where they had no representation impinged on their freedom. In addition, in the several interchanges within their "families" and at the town hall meetings, the students developed the procedures for telling the story of what had occurred, for engaging in deliberative processes, and for arguing with authorities about changes in policy. All these procedures transfer to other occasions, whether in other simulations or in other academic situations.

Reading the thoughts of some of the central historical figures and studying some of our own constructed reports during the course of the simulation, combined with reflections on both the family and town hall discussions, serve to introduce students to some tough questions that persist today: Why would anyone want a strong central government? How much power should any central government have? Do we need an extensive military force? Does a strong standing army pose a threat to individual liberty? How could you cite laws of nature to advance the cause of freedom and still protect the institution of slavery? What is the role of women in a land that pretends to be free and independent? What should be the extent of the bond among all colonies? Are taxes necessary? When do they become excessive or oppressive? During the course of our discussions about the problems facing Elmtown, we touched on these questions; but we can also see possibilities for addressing these contemporary issues directly in school/college forums that can offer potential for other schools, whether or not teachers rely on simulations like Colonial Elmtown.

CHAPTER 4

Living in Pre-Revolutionary War America: Colonial Elmtown

The resources in this chapter will support teachers in the effort to replicate the Colonial Elmtown experience with their own students. In its essence, the activity amounts to a series of discussions (family meetings and town hall deliberations). We chose to hold eight such discussions, but teachers who are pressed for time could use fewer by focusing on selected events or by combining events. The activity does, however, lend itself to a series of discussions so that students can experience the cumulative effect of increasingly provocative and oppressive actions by the British government. The idea here is for students to experience enough to be able to explain to someone else why there was an effort to break from Great Britain and risk fortunes, reputations, and lives in a Revolutionary War. Students need to experience several events in order to have a sense of why colonists were emboldened to face the greatest military force in the world and embark on an uncertain political experiment. Of course, students will learn much more than an accounting of the events that led to war. They will learn about key figures in the rebellion and about some political concepts and issues that continue to be debated today. They will also learn some important procedures for writing and for the critical and close reading of primary source texts.

In Chapter 3 we shared samples of classroom talk and students' writing to show what the simulation looks and sounds like in action. Most of the material that follows is addressed to the students who will participate in the activities. We have inserted notes to the teacher to suggest how to use the materials and implement the activity. Table 4.1 offers a capsule overview of the whole activity.

A NOTE ABOUT THE "GAME"

We have enacted Colonial Elmtown as a simulation game, with families earning credit for carrying out several responsibilities. We have found that students get swept up by the spirit of the simulation and worry little about earning game credit and positioning themselves ahead of others. While we

Table 4.1. Overview of the Colonial Elmtown Simulation

Phase	Actions	Outcomes
I. Inventing the family	• Students read books and view websites that describe their family's trade/profession. • Students select individual roles and negotiate relationships within the group (father, mother, grandma, etc.). • Students construct their family's narrative (origins, time in Elmtown, etc.). • Student envision their own home and the design of the town and its position in the colony.	Students write descriptions and narratives in journals. Some students produce floor plans and maps to reveal where they live and how they live.
II. Contending with events	• At each stage, the class reads the description of the current event (e.g., Stamp Act, Quartering Act), clarifying the actions and their implications. • Each family discusses how the event affects their lives and the community as a whole. • Family representatives join the town hall meeting: discovering a chance occurrence (spring floods, crime spree, etc.—an optional element), reporting the current event, discussing the impact, and searching for appropriate responses.	Each student writes a journal reflection: What has occurred? How has the event affected the family and community? What has the community decided? What feelings or reactions does the writer have about the recent events? A team of students produces a "consensus report," which can take one of many forms (e.g., a letter of protest, a pamphlet, an editorial, an open letter to organize a boycott).

have attended mostly to the substance of the quick give-and-take of the meetings, to the neglect of the counting of game credit, we expect that other, more accomplished bookkeepers (like our students) can take greater care, or devise systems to monitor one another's accomplishments.

As with all inquiries, the process begins with a compelling problem. We have found that students recognize and appreciate the problem when they see it represented in a narrative that reveals the current or potential harms and describes the people who might be threatened, the competing sides of the problems, and other complicating details that both support problem

Table 4.1. Overview of the Colonial Elmtown Simulation *(continued)*

Phase	Actions	Outcomes
III. Sharing a personal response	• Each student writes a summary response (e.g., a narrative of the sequence of events in the life of the family and town, an explanation of how the town functions through the democratic processes of the town hall meetings, a persuasive appeal to the king or Parliament to change policy and ease oppression). • Through the composing process, students plan, draft, share with classmates, and confer with the teacher.	Students produce narratives, letters, or reports.
IV. Acting as a historian (optional)	• The class studies the "History Sleuth" prompt, clarifying the task and the standard for historical analysis. • Students study the competing views of events. • Working collaboratively and independently, students write an analysis of two texts.	Students produce a written analysis of two texts that offer competing views of the events that the Elmtown community has experienced.

solving and defy simple solutions. With our classes, the following brief narrative introduces the simulated environment, the general problem, and the rules for play.

THE ELMTOWN NARRATIVE

In many ways, during Colonial times the residents of Elmtown, Massachusetts, enjoyed a comfortable life, although everyone worked hard and faced some tough winters. The residents enjoyed many freedoms, as they would expect as subjects of the English monarch. Freedom was a given for most settlers of European descent in North America, and being residents in a colony an ocean away from ruling powers in Europe, they became quite self-sufficient and somewhat independent.

Elmtown had six (or more) most influential families who worked together for the common good of the town. They didn't always agree, but they

settled their differences civilly through the discussions that occurred during
regular town hall meetings. These meetings were especially important during
times of crisis. After periods of lively exchanges at these meetings, the residents were usually able to compromise and act as one in the end.

While every year confronts the town with many difficulties—illnesses,
severe weather, poor crops, and even occasional lawbreaking—recently the
challenges have become more of an *economic* and *political* nature. If the
residents can continue to compromise and act as a singular force, the community should be able to survive and thrive. If the residents refuse compromise, remaining stubborn and contentious, they will splinter and destroy the
unified spirit of the community.

> *Goal*: Your goal as a member of the community is to achieve
> agreement on the actions that the unified residents should take in
> response to some significant problems. *In the end, everyone wins if
> the town remains unified, but unity will be the product of your work
> together to reach agreement on what action to take.*

> *Family Goal*: In helping to achieve the town goal, you can also
> win points for your own family by staying true to the strengths of
> your family. *In other words, the behavior of your family has to stay
> consistent with the identity and assigned strengths of your family.*

STAGES OF PLAY

There are several stages in the life of Colonial Elmtown. At each stage, each
family must discuss and agree about how they will represent the interests
of the family during the town meeting. At each town meeting, the residents
discuss the current crisis, evaluate the possible responses to the crisis, and
attempt to reach agreement (i.e., reach *consensus*). If the participants in a
town hall meeting cannot reach consensus, they can decide to meet again to
discuss the same crisis. The town residents reveal their agreement in a written *consensus report* authored by a team of students (usually one "family").
In each instance the team expresses their opinion of events and recommends
a course of action in regard to the current crisis.

While we offer examples of eight stages below, we can imagine a class
expanding the game, in the way that some video games allow for the player
to add levels or stages. As the life of Colonial Elmtown progresses, representatives from the families can introduce new stages by alerting the town
about crises that the other family members may not have been aware of.
These new stages should be consistent with the actual history of the colony.
Carefully researched suggestions can be submitted to the facilitator of the
town hall meetings for consideration.

At each stage in the life of Colonial Elmtown, families receive some communication from a sympathetic resident of one of the colonies. These different forms of communication (e.g., letters from a Pennsylvania farmer, reports on events in Boston, broadsides against Parliament) will reveal how other people have reacted to the current crisis. Representatives from the families find it useful to quote from such communications during town hall meetings, especially if they are quoting a highly respected authority (e.g., Patrick Henry, Samuel Adams, John Adams) who could influence others. Students also refer to the current pamphlets and newspaper articles that the teacher has circulated around the Elmtown community.

PROCEDURES

The game is not unstructured play, but conforms to a set of procedures for functioning in a team, contributing to the town hall meetings, and recording events and writing analyses. Some of the procedures involve preparation for the main event. The procedures for discussions within each family are similar to the procedures for discussions at the town hall meetings. We offer below the general guidelines as we address them to the students.

Forming a Family Identity: In your initial meeting as a family, you will need to do the following: (1) Study your role description, with special attention to your *strengths* and *interests*; (2) decide on a *family name*; (3) pick a *symbol* to represent who you are as a family (e.g., *fish, hammer, plow*); (4) decide on the members of the family (e.g., father, mother, grandma, daughter, son); and (5) decide who will be the primary spokesperson for the family at the town hall meetings. You might have a primary spokesperson and an alternate, or you might work on changing the rules for spokespersons, but you would have to get everyone at a town hall meeting to agree to a change to the established procedures.

Family Procedures: Each person in the family should be allowed and encouraged to contribute by offering solutions and by politely evaluating the suggestions of others. After weighing all the possible solutions, the family must agree on a recommended course of action and the rationale for that action. When the members of the family cannot agree, the head of the household must make the final decision and take this decision to the town hall meeting.

Town Hall Meeting Procedures: Town hall meetings are distinguished by their *civility* and *reason*. It is important to follow the procedures strictly, in order to accomplish the *town goal* and to earn **credit for your family.**

- Typically, the participants at town hall meetings in Colonial Elmtown were male landowners. *Only one spokesperson* from each family can participate in the meetings, although it is possible that a persuasive family could help the residents break with tradition and change past practice.
- For each meeting, a different spokesperson (representative from a family) *initiates the conversation*. Your family gets **credit** for initiating the conversation by summarizing the current problem, recommending a course of action, and supporting the recommendation by noting related information and explaining the significance of the information.
- Each speaker gets to speak his (or her) mind, *without interruption*. Everyone will have a chance to speak, so it is important to be patient until your turn comes, even if the speaker says something provocative, or even inflammatory. A family can **lose credit** for interrupting.
- After a participant has initiated the town hall meeting, the speaker who follows cannot offer an argument or make a suggestion without first *summarizing what the previous speaker has said* and checking that this summary is accurate. The speaker's family gets **credit** for doing this well.
- Only *one family representative* gets to speak at the town hall meeting, although it is possible to send notes to the speaker. A family can **lose credit** when someone who is not the designated representative intrudes on the meeting. As the town hall meetings continue, it is possible to refine the protocol, even allowing the substitution of one family member for another.
- Each speaker must remain *consistent to his or her identity* and take advantage of assigned strengths. Families earn **credit** when their spokesperson remains true to the family identity and strengths.
- The family earns **credit** only when all the members of the family write a diary entry for each stage. The diary entry will help to confirm the number of credits the family has earned. You will also want to have substantial content in your diary about the current events and the essence or outcomes of the family and town meeting discussions in order to have much to draw from in writing your final reflection.
- The participants in the town hall meeting need to arrive at *unanimous agreement*. You do not settle matters simply by taking a vote, and the majority cannot force the minority to agree. Agreement is sometimes achieved by compromise. **All families win when there is agreement.** Since the crises are immediate, timely, and significant, the group needs to act within a strict time limit.

- At the end of each town hall meeting, the group must *decide upon the appropriate action in response* to the problem. All families must contribute in order to earn **credit**. A team of students will volunteer to put the response into writing, whether it takes the form of a letter or a pamphlet or an editorial to solicit sentiments and support.
- In brief, the town "wins" when the residents agree on a response to at least six of the eight crises and produce a written response in the form of a consensus report to *all* crises.

LIVING AND RECORDING DAILY LIFE

While significant political events sometimes cause upheaval in the relative harmony and tranquility of the town, the residents also face other unpleasantness and occasional calamities, such as sickness, crime, bad weather, or accidents. For the most part, town hall meetings focus on the most immediate political problem. These events strike the town every day in a random way, following the toss of six dice: one from each family. The combined points on the dice will correspond to a numbered chance occurrence on a list (Appendix G). Identification and possible attention to these random occurrences begin each meeting.

We suggest that a teacher might find it useful to post a chart in the classroom to show the progress of each family and the whole town in earning credits toward their goals. Each family must earn at least *eight credits*, and the town must earn at least *six,* in order to be considered successful. The family emblem might appear on the wall chart to help track the family performance and allow an immediate measure of the current position relative to the goals of the game, just as one would be aware of progress in a video game.

DOCUMENTING COLONIAL LIFE

As a means for making meaning of the experience and collecting notes to support a summative response, we expect students to record events and their reactions at every stage. The journal entries record what has occurred at each stage, including the each day's calamity and the current political crisis. Volunteer teams of students produce "consensus reports" as the community's reactions to current events. In the end, we expect each student to write a summative composition that synthesizes everything that has occurred across the several stages.

1. Each student keeps a diary that records the significant conversations within the family and the critical crises facing the whole community. For each diary entry, the student describes what the crisis was, reports the major considerations that came up during the family discussion and the town hall meeting, and explains the action the community took and why. As the game progresses, it is helpful for each student to note what "worked" for the family during a town hall meeting and what adjustments had to be made to their strategies from one stage to another. We hope this reflection on what "worked" will build awareness of logic and rhetoric.

2. For each crisis situation, the town as a whole produces a written response. Each family contributes to this written response, but the primary responsibility will fall to a different family in each instance. The written response often takes the form of a letter, sometimes addressed to King George III and sometimes to the members of the British Parliament. The written response could also be a pamphlet, petition, or letter to a newspaper editor to circulate among the population, with the intention of winning support for your town's unified position.

3. At the end of the simulation, after experiencing all the crises, each resident will draw from all the written records, including the available primary source texts, in order to write a *summary report* on the town's Colonial experience. We have allowed students to choose any *one* of four forms: (1) Tell the story of what Elmtown experienced, including the significant events and the town's reaction to the events; (2) write an appeal to King George III or to his Parliament to describe the difficulties that the residents have experienced, how they responded to the difficulties, and what they are likely to do next; (3) in a letter to a cousin who lives in England but considers emigrating to North America, explain what this family member is likely to encounter by pointing to examples of what you have had to face and endure; or (4) in a letter to a friend who lives in another colony where town hall meetings are a foreign idea, explain how the town hall meetings in Elmtown function. For this last text, explain the process and describe the skills and attitudes that the town residents have to have in order for the town meetings to work. Help your friend make sense of the process by noting the example of at least one crisis when the town meeting functioned well. You could also illustrate by pointing to a meeting when the process and the outcome did not go so well. *You will be receiving detailed instructions for the writing that you choose to do.*

FORMING THE FAMILIES

Part of the fun for students comes in the inventing of the families. We take care in determining the membership of each family. In grouping students together, we take into account the particular characteristics of each student. We have found that four is a reasonable number to represent a family unit and to capitalize on various viewpoints. We hope to equip each group with a student who can assume leadership responsibilities. We also try to build in supports for English language learners or other students who face learning challenges.

The following descriptors provide the general guidelines for forming the family identities. At the beginning of the simulation, we share readings about various trades and occupations during Colonial times so that students have some historical basis for inventing themselves. While we assign the general identities (landowner, printer, innkeeper, etc.), students add to these by noting the specific ages, relationships, and special qualities among the members of the family. Even with the autonomy to invent the details, students stay true to the general guidelines. We offer six possibilities for family identities below, but a teacher could easily add to these possibilities.

1. Farmer/Small Landowner: You and your family work a small farm that you own. The farm allows you to produce some foods that you preserve for your own consumption, and you sell some grain, squash, milk, cheese, and eggs to earn the cash that you need for purchasing goods that you cannot produce on your own, including tea. You also need money to pay taxes. You know that there is a lot of unsettled land in the far western reaches of the colony, and you hope to move your family there someday to claim a broader expanse of land to produce a larger crop and earn more money. The great hope for your family and the promise implied by your presence in North America is that you could greatly advance your prosperity and your station in life, if only you could obtain more land from the far reaches of the colony, where vast tracts of land seem available for the taking.

2. Blacksmith: You have spent your entire adult life in Elmtown. You are proud of your trade and of your fine family. Your trade requires demanding physical labor and a good bit of artistry, which few people really understand or appreciate. The operation of a blacksmith's shop requires the investment in some essential equipment and access to the raw materials (e.g., lead and iron) that are necessary for the trade. You are committed to Elmtown and plan to stay there for the remainder of your life.

3. Lawyer/Large Landowner: Although your trade is the law, you also own extensive lands because your ancestors were some of the first settlers in the colony. Of course, you are rather a gentleman farmer and don't actually work the land yourself. You rent parcels of land to others who grow the crops and take only a small percentage. Through this arrangement you have become quite wealthy. Your wealth helps you to be an influential figure in the town. You know that as a landowner your status in the community is far above that of the mere renters, clerks, and tradespeople who also live in your town.

4. Shopkeeper: You are part of an emerging merchant class in the community, which means that you are wealthier than most. Your wealth depends on your being able to continue to receive goods from England. You can find local suppliers for much of what you sell, but the more luxurious items, like sugar, molasses, linen, and tea, come from England. You know also that distillers in your colony rely on an abundance of molasses to be able to produce the rum that is popular in your shop and at the inn. You make your greatest profit in selling some basic goods, and you hope to continue.

5. Fisherman: The father of this fisherman came to Massachusetts from Scotland, which he referred to as the "Kingdom of Scotland." He never supported the unification of Scotland and England as "Great Britain" and longed for a free and independent Scotland. He came to North America in order to seek a sense of freedom from government intrusion and the feeling of independent, unfettered living. This Scottish father liked to quote these lines from the Scottish poet Robert Burns:

Wha for Scotland's king and law
Freedom's sword will strongly draw,
Freeman stand or freeman fa'—
Let him follow me!

The family continues to value freedom and independent thinking. Among the townspeople of Elmtown, the fisherman is probably the most *passionate* and will not stand for the government's intrusion in the family's affairs. The ocean separates this family from the king of England, and that separation is a physical reminder of true independence.

6. Innkeeper: The inn at Elmtown serves as a hotel, restaurant, tavern, and tearoom. As innkeepers, the members of this family play host to travelers and to the town's residents. Travelers on their way to Boston often stop at the inn. As you know, Boston has become a hotbed of radical thought and action, and sometimes the radical thinkers pass through your inn. A key to maintaining customer loyalty is being pleasant, polite, and amiable. The innkeeper has become quite adept at serving as a mediator in many disputes. His intervention has stopped many a brawl in his inn. He has not had strong political views, seeking to find the middle ground between extremes.

STAGES OF POLITICAL DEVELOPMENT IN ELMTOWN

The experience in Colonial Elmtown involves multiple stages, some of which can be combined for consideration together. At the beginning, we alert students to the notion that, guided by their own research and related reading, any family might devise another stage, which a student can describe and offer to the teacher for consideration. We offer eight stages here, in language directed to the students. At each stage, we ask the families to consider two questions and to be prepared to share their responses at the next town hall meeting.

Stage 1: England's victory in the French and Indian War (known in Europe as the "Seven Years' War") has given England dominance in North America. At the same time, the war has left England 140 million pounds in debt. By some calculations, converted to modern dollars, this debt would be somewhere near *$770 million* (you might want to calculate this yourself to get a sense of the extent of the debt). England has been at war with other European nations for decades, and the expense of war has added up. In addition, King George III and the Parliament of Britain have kept soldiers in the colonies to protect residents, who are English subjects, from attacks from Indians who had allied with the French. The king and Parliament need a way to reduce further costs and to pay down the debt. The king has issued a proclamation (known as the Proclamation of 1763) that would prohibit the residents of the colonies from moving into western lands that the king had determined would be reserved for the native tribes of North America. Any landowner who had hoped to extend his land holdings farther would be prohibited from doing so. In addition, the king and Parliament introduced a series of new taxes on sugar, molasses, and other "luxury" items. The new taxes were grouped together under the informal title of "the Sugar Act." The new taxes would make matters difficult for everyone, but especially for merchants and innkeepers, because the increased costs for these items would discourage people from buying them. The most irritating part of the Sugar Act was that Massachusetts and the other colonies had no representative in the British Parliament to argue against the act or to vote against it.

Stage 2: King George III and the British Parliament have issued the Quartering Act. The king has maintained a military presence in the colonies to protect his subjects. Keeping an army equipped, housed, and fed so far from home has become increasingly costly. Part of the solution is to direct the colonists to house soldiers in their homes. This means that each resident would have to provide sleeping accommodations for some soldiers when the soldiers are stationed in the area. You understand further that in some instances the soldiers have expected their hosts to feed them and to launder their clothes. An innkeeper who has several rooms would have to surrender some rooms to soldiers when ordered. You have heard that the Colonial legislature in New York agreed on a proclamation to condemn the Quartering Act and refuse to allow soldiers into the homes of New York residents. It is hard to imagine, however, how the residents will resist the orders of men with guns. In response to the proclamation, the king disbanded the Colonial legislature in New York and has threatened to dissolve other legislative bodies across the colonies.

Stage 3: Still looking for new revenues to pay down the war debt, King George III and the English Parliament have issued the Stamp Act, which requires colonists to pay a fee (a kind of tax) to have an official stamp placed on certain documents that are exchanged among residents. These "documents" include playing cards, mortgages, patent medicines, contracts, and newspapers. The sentiment in your town has been a willingness to pay "internal" taxes. *Internal* refers to taxes that residents discussed among themselves and have agreed to pay for the benefit of their own local community. But across several colonies, residents have resisted what they consider "external" taxes—those imposed on them by a British Parliament where you have no representative who can argue for your interests and vote one way or the other. For most citizens, the new tax represented by the Stamp Act will be an inconvenience. For lawyers, it will be a headache, because they deal with nothing but legal documents that require the stamp. For many merchants, the tax will make it even more difficult to operate their small businesses. You understand that several of the colonies have proposed to meet in New York City to form a Stamp Act Congress. The delegates to the Congress would compose a "Declaration of Rights and Grievances" to send to Parliament and the king. This is a rather radical step, one that some people would consider treasonous because it involves resistance to the king's orders. You have learned that one of the more radical delegates to the Congress wants to make this statement in the declaration: "*Resolved,* therefor that the General Assembly of this Colony have the only and exclusive Right and Power to lay Taxes and Impositions upon the inhabitants of this Colony and that every Attempt to vest such Power in any person or persons whatsoever other than the General Assembly aforesaid has a manifest Tendency to destroy British as well as American Freedom." That says that the king has no right to impose a tax without the consent of the colonists. Such a bold affront is likely to anger the king and inflame some members of Parliament.

Stage 4: Determined to find new taxes to generate revenue to pay down the war debt, the king and the British Parliament have issued the "Townshend Acts." These acts impose on the colonists taxes on lead, paint, glass, and tea. The costs of these items will obviously increase, making the quality of living in Massachusetts more strained. The taxes on lead, paint, and glass will especially affect some merchants and craftspeople. The tax on tea will affect every household in Elmtown, where most residents come from an English tradition of daily tea consumption. With the new tax, some residents may no longer be able to afford tea. These new taxes have been added to a series of other taxes, and they all add to mounting costs for all residents. The disturbing part of the new taxes is that no one from Massachusetts or any other colony serves in the British Parliament. These new taxes, then, are further examples of "external" taxes that no affected colonist had an opportunity to vote on.

Stage 5: You learned today that there is an organized resistance to the taxes that you have to pay for goods imported from England. You have to pay taxes on tea, paint, glass, lead, playing cards, and other imports only if you actually *purchase* them. It follows that the way to resist the taxes is to refuse to buy any of the imports. People across the several colonies have agreed to avoid buying English imports of any kind, or to "boycott" them. Since there is a big market for English goods in the colonies, the boycott would cause economic distress for the English government and a hardship for the companies sending the goods to North America. When the businesses are hurting, they will put pressure on Parliament to change the taxes—at least, that's the way it is supposed to work in theory. And the boycott will work only if *everyone agrees* not to buy English goods. There has to be agreement among all residents not to buy English imports, even if this resistance causes inconvenience and personal hardship.

Stage 6: You just learned some disturbing news from the Massachusetts capital of Boston. Recognizing that the colonists were becoming increasingly resistant and militant, the king sent more British troops to Boston, which seems to be a hotbed of resistance. The presence of the British army in the streets of Boston further infuriated many of the residents, who pelted the soldiers with rocks and called them insulting names. The British soldiers responded by opening fire on a crowd of Bostonians. They killed three immediately and wounded eleven others. Among the eleven wounded, two later died. The dead included Boston residents Crispus Attucks, Samuel Gray, and James Caldwell. A witness to the shooting drew a picture of the scene and labeled it the "Boston Massacre." A local silversmith named Paul Revere engraved the image from the drawing so that a printer could make many copies for circulating, and some copies have reached Elmtown. Your fellow colonists from Boston look to you for a strong denunciation directed at General Thomas Gage, a commander of the British forces in North America. In such a letter, representing the opinion of all of the residents of your town, you would point out that the actions of the British soldiers were cowardly, improvident, and unjust. Before composing such a letter, you will need to see the full report about the "massacre" so that you are sure that you are not making false accusations.

Stage 7: King George III has recognized that a number of ships from the colonies have been able to smuggle British goods into the colonies without paying the proper taxes. The King and Parliament were also upset when a band of militant Bostonians boarded a British merchant vessel in the night and dumped several crates of expensive tea into the waters of Boston Harbor. When Parliament issued a series of acts in response to the smuggling and the "Tea Party," the colonists began to refer to the legislation as the "Coercive Acts" and the "Intolerable Acts." For one thing, the king closed Boston Harbor. No ships could dock in Boston to unload needed goods or to load goods for sale in Europe. The closing of the harbor would have dire consequences for merchants and for other citizens throughout Massachusetts. The new acts also made it possible for British military to board any ship or enter any home to search it for weapons or for smuggled goods. This is an outrage to British subjects, who like to believe that they live under the rule of law where citizens and their property would not be searched without a proper warrant. The right to privacy seems to apply only to subjects in Britain and not in the colonies. Some residents of Boston think it is time for more radical action, including *sabotage* of British ships and military installations. Some Bostonians have urged the residents of Elmtown to join them in these covert acts in defiance of the king.

Stage 8: Many people from across the 13 colonies have found the actions of the king and his Parliament to be intolerable. Leaders from these colonies have called for the formation of a Continental Congress that would support a united response to the king and Parliament. The proposed Congress would meet at Carpenter's Hall in Philadelphia and produce a petition addressed to the king. The petition would list all the grievances suffered by the colonists and would threaten a unified boycott against British goods and against goods from any British colonies outside North America. The members of the Congress would represent the people of their home colonies, and their names would appear on the document that harshly criticized the king, possibly leaving them vulnerable to retaliation. Elmtown could send a representative to the Congress in Philadelphia, or could send a letter of support to the Congress in general so that the representatives would know that they had the backing of the people of the colonies.

PREPARING FOR THE TOWN HALL MEETING

In preparation for the town hall meeting, the teacher distributes the written description of the current crisis and reads the description aloud, in some instances glossing the vocabulary, adding some details, and clarifying what has happened. The family members then tackle the problem by judging how it will affect them and the other members of their community. We build in at least one loyalist each time we do the simulation. We want this element of dissent to complicate the town hall meetings and generate genuine dialogue.

As the families discuss the current event and ponder how it affects them, the teacher circulates from group to group to monitor the discussion, challenge some suggested action, and add details for consideration. For example, the innkeeper might worry that the quartering of soldiers might cut into his or her profits. Other families might seem less affected, until the teacher suggests that some of the common British were recruited from prisons and from the lowest elements in society. This detail makes the problem more acute and provokes some families to seek an immediate and vigorous resolution.

MOVING INTO THE TOWN HALL

We like to provoke students at the initial meeting by noting that in Colonial times it was common for the male head of the household to represent the family at the town hall meetings. In the contemporary classroom, this constraint is met with strong opposition, at least from the girls. Our first order of business, then, is to determine the rules about who can speak and how we can alternate speakers in the least disruptive way. The students deliberate and arrive at consensus about the protocol before we move on to the issues with the king and Parliament.

In addition to the political events and economic conditions that affect the residents of Elmtown, these colonists face the dangers and random occurrences that could befall any community, such as bad weather, fires, crime, and illness. A representative from each of the six families rolls one die, and the combined points across the six dice will reveal one of the occurrences listed in Appendix G. The teacher/facilitator who reads the description can insert the name of a specific family to indicate who specifically is affected.

A teacher can obviously omit this part of the simulation, but we have found that students enjoy this element, which adds a bit of suspense and complication to the proceedings. We list the "random occurrences" in Appendix G.

We do want to emphasize that the discussions serve at least three functions: First, students grapple with the events of history in an effort to understand the effect of events and to gain insight into the motivations for the actions of the principal players in the historical drama. Second, students read primary source texts to learn about the reactions of colonists at the time and to summarize their arguments, especially in support of their own. The discussions and the related work with the primary source texts position students to read other texts, including historical fiction, from an informed and empathic position. Third, students practice the many procedures that transfer to their writing: telling what happened, connecting events to explain causes, arguing for specific courses of action, paraphrasing and evaluating what other thinkers say, and summarizing a body of information.

WRITTEN RESPONSE TO COLONIAL ELMTOWN

By the time that students have finished discussing the several stages of their Colonial experience, they have a lot to say, and they have had practice saying what has occurred, how it has affected the community, and what they should do about it. Now is the time to put everything together in a written response. We offer the following prompts to direct students in their effort, and we suggest that the rubric that appears in Appendix C can guide students' efforts and provide the criteria for providing feedback. We accompany each prompt with this note: "Be sure to share your plan and your draft with other writers so that you can know how your composition affects them and so that you have corrected any errors in order to make your work as clear as possible for its intended audience." The admonition aligns with our practice of guiding students through a structured process of development of their work, anticipating that they will share with a peer, conference with the teacher, or both.

PROMPTS FOR WRITING

We like to give students some choice for their written responses to the simulation. The choices allow students to tell the story of their experience, explain how colonists lived or how the town hall meetings function as democracy in action, or appeal to the king or Parliament for relief from policies that have affected lives in the colony. While each kind of writing can be quite distinct, we rely on general standards for good writing to serve as a basis for assessment and feedback, valuing especially a unified focus, logical development, cohesive ties, accuracy and relevancy in reporting events, organization, and developmentally appropriate precision in the conventions of language. The four choices follow.

1. Tell the *story* of what Elmtown experienced, including the significant events and the town's reaction to the events. Tell the story in the sequence as it happened. What were the important events? How did events affect families? How did the events affect the community as a whole? As you would in writing any good story, be sure that your story has these important elements:

   • A clear sense of the setting so that the reader can imagine what the place and time were like.

- Characters who are brought to life so that a reader can imagine them, including hearing what they say and how they say it.
- A series of events that are easy to follow in sequence so that a reader can see the connections between the events.
- A sequence of events that follows a central conflict in a pattern that leads to a climax, dramatic moment, or resolution.

2. Write an *appeal* to King George III or to his Parliament to describe the difficulties that the residents have experienced, how they responded to the difficulties, and what they are likely to do next. At the time of the last stage of Colonial Elmtown, the colonies were still tied to Great Britain and had not engaged in any hostilities. Your appeal should make a case for a change in the actions of the king and Parliament so that everyone can avoid violence or separation from the home country. As with any persuasive letter sent to an authority, you will want to choose your language carefully and make sure that your letter contains the following elements:

- An introduction to remind the king about the central problem between his government and the colonies in America. This introduction will include your briefly stated recommendation about what the king should do.
- A recounting in detail about the injustices and abuses that the residents of Elmtown have accused the king and Parliament of. You will need to be very specific about the actions of the king and Parliament and about how the actions have harmed people in your town and colony.
- A summary of the actions that the residents of Elmtown have already taken to get some help in relieving them of the burdens that they have suffered for many years.
- A repeated summary of the central problem and your recommendation for change.

3. In a *letter to a cousin* who lives in England but considers immigrating to North America, *explain* what this family member is likely to encounter by pointing to examples of what you have had to face and endure. Your cousin has already written to you to ask about your impressions, and your cousin expects a response. Your letter to your cousin should contain the following elements:

- An introduction that acknowledges that you know what the audience wants to know.
- A detailed description of what life has been like in Elmtown. Your descriptions should recall political events, financial or economic challenges, and physical hardships. Your cousin will be unfamiliar

with much of what you have experienced and will need to know in detail what your life is like.

- Highlights both of the positive experiences and the potential, as well as any significant difficulties.
- A summary that recalls why the cousin wrote, and what you would recommend.

4. In a letter to a friend who lives in another colony where town hall meetings are a foreign idea, explain how the town hall meetings in Elmtown function. Explain the process and describe the skills and attitudes that the town residents have to have in order for the meetings to work. Help your friend make sense of the process by noting the example of at least one crisis when the meeting functioned well. You could also illustrate by pointing to a meeting when the process and the outcome did not go so well. In the letter, include:

- An introduction that acknowledges that you know what the audience wants to know.
- A detailed description of the process of facing crises and solving problems in town hall meetings in Elmtown. Your descriptions should recall specific events and note how the residents worked together to figure out what to do. Did people always agree? If you didn't agree, how did you settle your differences?
- A summary statement that reviews the process and makes a recommendation about what residents should do in your friend's town.

BE A HISTORY SLEUTH: AN OPTIONAL EXTENSION

We expect that the Colonial Elmtown simulation will place students in the position of residents of a pre–Revolutionary War town, allowing them to experience the events that led to war and a declaration of independence. A teacher can also ask students to assume the role of a historian who examines competing accounts of events and evaluates the accuracy of each account to advance a synthesized interpretation of history. In order to do this, each student would have to have substantial knowledge of events, knowledge gained largely through the simulated experiencing of those events. The complete prompt and related documents appear in Appendix F. Here is the basic task:

Your Job as a History Sleuth

On the attached pages, you will find letters exchanged between two cousins, one an American living in Boston and the other his English counterpart living in Manchester, England. Your job as a history sleuth is to *judge the extent to which each writer accurately represents the events that led to the War for Independence or American Revolutionary War.*

The two histories of the events come in the form of letters between cousins, one in Massachusetts and one in Manchester, England. We expect that students would make their own individual effort to study the two letters and judge the merit of each account, but students also benefit from further collaboration. The task is not a matter of deciding which letter writer is right and which is wrong. As Georgina shows through her response in Chapter 3, the outcome is a written analysis that acknowledges some accuracies and recognizes some dubious reports in each account. Georgina doesn't blindly choose sides, but offers a third account, acknowledging merit where merit exists, and offering her own unique insights. When students experience the simulation as a game, they "win" or achieve success when they collaborate and produce a product that has improved as a result of dialogue with peers and with other writers, both past and present. This "History Sleuth" extension of the simulation emphasizes that students apply procedures that will be of use to them again and again in thinking about problems and writing about historical and literary texts. The "Road from Appomattox" simulation described in the next two chapters requires students again to read, summarize, and evaluate a series of epistolary texts, leading to a summative assessment of the experience of war and its lingering effects.

CHAPTER 5

Reflecting on the Effects of War

In a simulation game we call "Road from Appomattox," which we share in detail in Chapter 6, we asked students to imagine what it would be like to travel home from Appomattox Court House, Virginia, after General Lee had surrendered to General Grant. Although some fighting continued in other arenas, the war was essentially over; it was time to reflect on the carnage and deprivations of the previous years and to recognize the difficulties that lay ahead. While there was certainly relief at the end of armed conflict, the journey home and the renewal of individuals' lives would be arduous, sometimes full of uncertainty and sometimes full of hope and possibility. Table 5.1 projects the entire sequence and suggests what a teacher might look for before proceeding from one phase of the sequence to another.

Following the procedures of our Road from Appomattox simulation, Caroline read aloud to the class the letter that she and her "traveling" companions had received from a friend.

> *Caroline:* We received this letter from . . . my friend Beth. Here is what she says:
>
> Dear Friend,
>
> It is obvious that the soldiers involved in this devastating war have died and have suffered from horrible wounds and from deprivation. Few citizens realize the sacrifice made by brave women and men who have supported the troops.
>
> You and I both made the commitment to leave our comfortable homes to provide for the medical care of the sick and wounded troops during the war. Few people realize that approximately twice as many soldiers have died from disease than have died from wounds in battle. We have witnessed the horrible destruction of the war and the terrible wounds suffered by the brave soldiers.
>
> I have been inspired especially by the work of Dorothea Dix and Clara Barton, who have organized the efforts to bring sanitation and medical attention to the sick and wounded. At one time, people thought that women had no place near the front lines of battle, but the bravery of these women has affirmed for me that

Table 5.1. The Road from Appomattox Sequence

Phase	Actions	Outcomes
1. Forming the teams	• Students invent details of their identity. • Students select individual roles within the team and their relationships to one another. • Students construct their team's imagined roles in the simulation (family members, military friends, colleagues, etc.).	• Students write descriptions, narratives, and reflections in journals.
2. Contending with events	• Students read letters and a travel challenge. • Each team discusses how the travel challenge affects their progress on their journey home. • Each team comes to a decision in response to the travel challenge. • Each defends its decision against the opposition of critics.	• Each student writes a diary entry describing the travel challenge, summarizing the content of the letter and the team's reaction to the letter. • A team spokesperson reports to the entire class the team's decision and provides reasons for the decision.
3. Sharing a personal response	• Each student writes a summary response about the significant events on the trip, and a reflection on the overall effect that the Civil War had on people, the land, and the hope for the future. • Through the composing process, students plan, draft, share with classmates, and confer with the teacher.	• Students produce narratives or reports.

in the future there will be more opportunities than ever before for women.

> Your friend, Beth

Mrs. Galas: I understand that your team also faced some difficulty on the way home. Tell us about the current problem.

Clifford: We are supposed to carry a letter home from a dying soldier to his family. We will be passing near his home, but it will take us out of our way and delay us. We'll be delayed for a day. We talked it

over and we decided to keep going so we won't be delayed, and we
can mail the letter to the family later.

Filomena: Wait. You promised to deliver the letter? This was the dying
soldier's last request? How could you keep going?

Clifford: We figured that the letter is not going to bring him back, and
they are just as well off getting the bad news later.

Tyler: That's so . . . insensitive. They will know that the war is over,
but they won't know what happened to this soldier. It will only cost
you 1 day.

Mrs. Galas: The other groups seem rather critical of your decision.
Have you changed your mind?

Caroline: [Looking to her team members, who are shaking their heads
to indicate a negative reply] Uhhhh . . . Nah. I think we'll go on
and send the letter later.

In the Road from Appomattox simulation, we position students in the
moments following General Lee's surrender in April 1865. Six groups of
travelers work their way home. In other classrooms this might be seven or
eight groups. Their identities, conditions, and directions home are different. The simulation relies on a journey motif and a race format, with the
six groups vying with one another to be the first to reach home. We don't
reward the winners with a trophy or candy or grades, but rely on the race
format to add a dynamic to the sharing of communications and problem
solving. Students seem content simply to be declared the winners of the
race. As with the Colonial Elmtown experience that we describe in Chapter
4, the idea is to give students an extended experience in an imagined environment and have them record the events, review the decisions of their own
group and others, and reflect on the accumulated experience. One of the
attractions of the race motif is that students have to puzzle over some ethical
dilemmas, measuring their desire to win the race against demands for help,
concerns for safety, and respect for human dignity. While some groups are
initially driven to move forward at all costs, since it is a simulation game,
after all, they tend to become more reflective and empathic as the game progresses and their own imagined circumstances change.

We extend the "race" over 20 days, which we divide into five phases.
Of course, we do not work for an extended time on each of these 20 days;
on most days, we simply move the groups along the road unless some decision or chance calamity delays them. In each phase, students receive letters
from family or friends and face various dilemmas and random problems.
As with the vintage computer games *Oregon Trail* and *Amazon Trail* and a
previously reported "Bridger Trail" (McCann, 1996), the players' progress
will depend on the decisions they make and the resources they accumulate.
We like to post a 20-day timeline across the front of the room and have each
group of students construct an emblem to represent their team. Each team

posts its progress each day, moving its emblem forward one space with each class meeting, unless their decisions (e.g., delivering the last letter of a dying soldier) delay the group. While each team receives five letters and contends with five problems, a spokesperson reads each letter aloud. In the end, each student is exposed to 30 letters and 30 "travel challenges." As we show in Chapter 6, the letters and the dilemmas are rich with details about the war and the problems of reconstruction. As we show below, the students worked many of these details into their written reflections or fictional accounts of their experience.

One attraction for students is the arrival of mail at each turn. Each team receives an envelope that contains a letter and a description of a travel challenge. Each letter provides some insight into the causes of the war; the effects of the war; and the remaining economic, social, and political issues that confronted the nation in 1865, some of which continue to plague us today. On one level, the travel challenge poses a problem-solving opportunity for each group, and the tension between winning the race and doing what seems to be right contributes to the dynamic of the simulation. While students can have some engaging small-group conversations about their particular dilemma, the game calls for them to make matters public— to share with the whole class what they decided and how they came to their decision. As Nancy Galas demonstrates in the classroom interchange represented above, the rest of the class can judge the efficacy and the ethics of the decision, putting the team in a position to offer rational grounds for its decision.

WRITING ABOUT THE WAR AND RECONSTRUCTION

We want each student to reflect on the team's journey and on what he or she has learned from the letters and travel challenges of all the teams in the class. Journal writing offers a simple and authentic means for recording experience for later reflection. As in the Colonial Elmtown simulation, at each stage in the journey, we prompt the students to record what has happened. Here is how we prompted the journal writing throughout the simulation:

Journal Entry Prompt

Imagine that many years after the Civil War, historians and students will use your travel journal to reveal the *specific events* and *effects* of the war. Your journal will serve as a window to allow readers to look into the conditions in America from 1861 to 1865.

In your travel journal, write about the following:

- What have you learned about the suffering and destruction that have resulted from the war?

- What difficulties have you and your companions faced on your journey home?
- How did you and your companions resolve the difficulties or solve the problems that confronted you? Explain why you made the decisions you made, and describe the process you followed to make your decisions.
- What difficulties did other teams face, and how did they resolve problems and make decisions?
- What political, economic, and social problems connected to the war do the situations and experiences of the travelers reveal?

When the simulation was over and the members of each class "experienced" loss, horror, deprivation, grief, terror, injustice, heroism, triumph, defeat, and hope, they wrote their reflections on the war in one of three ways: a story about the journey and related events, a report on the causes and effects of the war, or an appeal to President Johnson to advise him about a spirit and path for reconciliation. The three prompts appear as Appendix H, "Writing About What You Have Learned."

Just as journals and peer dialogue were important to the writing process in the Colonial Elmtown simulation described in Chapters 3 and 4, the daily journal entries and peer interactions are also great supports to the writer in this simulation. The journals helped as a recorded source of information and reflection, but to respond to the prompts, the students had to do more than string a series of journal entries together in order to complete their final written reflections. Part of the composing process involved students' talking to their peers about what they were inclined to write and how they could execute a plan. While students continued to work in their assigned teams, they talked about the prospects for writing about any one of the prompts. We judge that by having the choice from three prompts, the students could select a mode of writing they felt comfortable with, yet each possibility served as a vehicle for revealing what they had learned. When they selected one possibility, they also talked about how they would gather and share information that would help them in the execution of the composition. As students began to draft, they shared their work with peers and with the teacher for feedback. Within some reasonable time constraints, the students continued to work on their compositions until they deemed them worthy of collecting in a class anthology for public viewing.

In our classes, we found that students were generally enthusiastic about writing about what they had learned. We judge that the students' confidence grew from their emerging sense of literacy competency built on earlier writing experiences during the school year. In fact, we confess that in some instances we encouraged students toward some kind of writing closure as soon as possible, because many of them were keen to refine and extend their writing well beyond our expectations.

We offer two compositions here—one a report and one a story. They are the product of drafting, reviewing with peers and a teacher, and reworking the compositions to greater and greater refinement. At the end of each composition we comment on the quality of the writing and what it reveals about what their authors learned about history during the simulation. We hope that the quality of the students' work makes you wonder how students were able to produce such elaborated writing, and we expect to satisfy that curiosity with the simulation materials that we share in Chapter 6. In that chapter we walk the reader through the simulation process and offer the resources necessary to replicate the experience or to design something similar to explore other concepts, issues, or periods of history.

A REPORT ON THE EFFECTS OF WAR

First we share excerpts from a rather straightforward expository report. The writer chose to focus on the effects of war and a projection of how the nation might proceed.

Effects of the Civil War

Eric Patterson

The Civil War caused many changes, good and bad. There were many hardships. The loss of loved ones, injuries, and disease are just to name a few. There was also plenty of hope, though.

The Civil War is over now. Many hardships lie ahead. The widows will have to work *very* hard even if they have no kids. The plantation owners can sell some of their land for profit. They can live off that for a while. With the competition for jobs, the aftermath of the Civil War looks like it will go pretty bad. The journey home, for the survivors, will be tough, too.

I think the economy won't change in the North. They will continue to have factories and be industrial. The South will probably continue to have many farms. However, the wealthy plantation owners will turn poor. What will probably happen is either rich Northerners will go South, buy the land, and have the Southerners work for them, or the South can trade in its Confederate money for American money. In the South, the economy will suffer. The Confederate money is now worthless. The competition for jobs will also cause people to have harsh lives. All the freed slaves will be looking for jobs, along with the Southerners who can't afford the land they own anymore.

There is plenty of hope for the freed slaves. It would seem like a good idea to go North, but staying South has good hope, too. If Northerners come South and buy the plantation land, the former slaves can work for them. That will save the time of traveling North. If they do travel North, they will probably make a small living. If they get promoted, they will make a good living and a happy life. There is hope for free men wherever they go.

The Civil War will cause the North and South to have more arguments. The South will want revenge because General Sherman set fire to so many buildings. The North will have a grudge against the South for wanting to secede and therefore "starting" the war. World War II started because Germany was mad about World War I. We're lucky there wasn't a Civil War II. The two sides won't be happy with each other. They will have the war of who's in the political seats. That will go on for a long time, and it still goes on today.

The Civil War did not only cause suffering. It also caused many advances. In the war, the U.S. used its first submarines. Also, some ships had iron sides that could resist cannonballs better than wood. Many prisoners of war were treated horribly. There will be rules for how to treat prisoners of war. If you compare the U.S.A.'s military from before to after, it will be weaker from loss of men in the beginning years. After about three years, it will be *way* stronger though. Women will also play a stronger role in supporting the war. They were often nurses or spies in the Civil War.

Hard times lay ahead for the U.S. There will be many sufferings. They will eventually get through, though.

Eric's writing reveals much about what he has learned about history and about writing. In this composition, supported in large measure by the many discussions and the related journal entries that preceded this report, Eric reveals his understanding of the distinctions between the economies and cultures of the North and South. He acknowledges and lists the consequences of war. He writes about the current and previous hardships and hopes. In his report, Eric organizes his writing in a way that would support most readers in following his discussion. He discusses the broader economic consequences and then turns his attention to the specific impact on the liberated slaves in the South. He demonstrates an understanding of some complex ideas about economic and political concepts when he characterizes economic conditions that the postwar nation faces. He cautions that resentment will linger on both sides, making reconstruction and cooperation difficult. He talks about the hopes of the freed slaves and the technical advances as a result of the war. He also anticipates future practices that derive from the war—such as the rules for exchange and treatment of prisoners, the roles and contributions of women, and provisions for a strong and stable military. Throughout the composition, Eric effectively supports his observations by citing relevant information drawn from written documents and discussion. Eric's composition also reveals the literacy and social studies overlap that the C3 Framework for Social Studies envisions: The clarity of his written expression depends on the accuracy and sufficient detail of his support. He connects effects to their related causes as he discusses social, economic, political, and military results of the war.

Certainly the report does not demonstrate an exhaustive knowledge of the causes of war, the events of 4 years of combat, or the effects of war. But this 5th-grader has shown a sophistication and depth of knowledge in his writing about the effects of war. The writing is organized, coherent, logical, and sufficiently thorough for the purposes of the current task. We know that Eric will study the Civil War again in 7th and 11th grade. Taken as evidence of proficiency in being able to connect events and draw logical conclusions and implications, Eric's report reveals him to be well-positioned to study other eras of history and examine experiences through political, economic, and social lenses. We judge also that this writing, along with the observations of Eric's interactions in his team and across whole-class discussions, is a much more reliable assessment of learning than the more conventional multiple-choice or short-answer tests.

A NARRATIVE REFLECTION ON EXPERIENCE

Our second example of a student's writing contrasts with Eric's more conventional academic report. Despite the different format, the writer incorporates many of the events identified in the simulation and uses those events to structure the arc of the narrative. The narrative reports events and implies an argument about the causes and effects of the war. Kathryn's story is quite lengthy, and we reproduce just a portion of it here to illustrate how she has woven together the events that she has "experienced."

Heading North—a story

Kathryn Hagstrom

"Mama!" I cried, while desperately struggling to work free of the white man's grip on my arm.

"No! Don't take her! Don't take my baby!" my mother screamed helplessly. Mama, me, and many other black men and women were standing on a platform, being auctioned off to the highest bidder.

"Anne." I heard a voice somewhere far away call my name. "Anne!" the faint voice called again. I turned to look where the voice had come from, but I saw no one. I turned my attention back to where the platform was, but it had been replaced by a large cotton field with many slaves pricking their hands on the sharps needles of the cotton plant. I felt my body start to shake. "Anne! You must wake up!"

"Come on Anne! We've got to hurry. The overseer says he's got to make an announcement. We're all to meet him at the fields['] beginning."

"Okay," I said as I rolled off my cot. We both walked out of the hut and started down the dirt path to the fields.

"So what were you dreaming about?" Susan laughed. "You were tossing and turning and you were making a pretty odd face."

"I was dreaming about the day I got taken away from my Mama," I told her.

"Oh," she said quietly "that one again."

Everyone immediately stopped their conversations when they heard the crunching of leaves under heavy field shoes. We all looked up to see the overseer with a look of pure hatred and loathing on his face.

"Get in a line!" he barked at us. We all scrambled quickly into a perfectly straight line. "It was bestowed upon me, the job of giving you your good news." He paused a moment to glare at us all. The overseer was a cruel man who hated all black people. If you even dared to put yourself out of line, the punishment was severe. "So," he continued begrudgingly, "as I'm sure you do not know, the Civil War has ended. That means, you are all free. You now have the choice of staying and working on the plantation, or leaving to go wherever you want." The overseer spat at these last words. "Those of you who want to leave, go and get you your things. NOW!!"

Me and Susan looked at each other. Without saying anything, we knew what we had to do. We must get away from here and be free. Susan and I, along with several other slaves began our journey back down the path to the huts, to get our things and begin our new lives as free people.

It has been about a day since we began our trip to the North. We've only had one meal so far and it was rabbit. All of us have been traveling for about an hour today, and by the sun's position in the sky I'd say it was late morning.

"Mama" one of the two children that were traveling with us said turning toward a tall muscular woman. "How much further till we get there?"

"Many days, my child. Many days," she said.

So, that night we all gathered around the young woman, Claire, to hear what her letter had to say. It turned out to be from her cousin Cyril. He talked of how people were dying because they were trying to teach Black people how to read. Then she said that he hoped that things would change for Black people now that the war was over.

He also said that he hoped that institutions would open one day where even black people can go and study. I personally hope that his predictions come true, and everyone can study together as equals.

After everything had been looked over we gathered around Claire to see what news she had for us. Today the letter was from her friend, Jacob. He said how there was segregation in the Union army. And how they were sending out whole troops of African Americans, instead of both white and black troops. Also many of the black troops were apparently getting the lesser equipment and that is why so many were dying. However my hopes are with Jacob's that one day both white and black people can fight side-by-side.

"Aaaaaaaah!" Sobbed the little boy. "It hurts!" I along with several other people have been working feverishly for the past five minutes to remove porcupine quills from a little boy's foot and shin. He apparently was walking along and saw a "weed." However, when he kicked the "weed," it turned out to be a porcupine. And now, of course, we have to get all the porcupine thorns out of him. "Please stop," he wailed. I couldn't imagine the pain he must feel. Those thorns were in deep.

After finally removing the thorns we all gave him a good lecture on why this was a good example of why he should think before he acts. But still, we had to delay another day in our journey so the boy's leg could get a bit better before he had to walk on it again. At least we've gotten to travel for almost a week since the last incident, I thought to myself.

So, after setting up camp we once again gathered around Claire to hear the news. This time it was from her friend Thaddeus. He said he was a soldier in a black regiment, and that he was involved in the Siege of Petersburg. He also said how there were extreme racial difference in the war too. He told in the letter of Grant's idea to dig a tunnel under the confederate line, so that the Union soldiers could come out and make a surprise attack on the Confederates. However, when they were using dynamite to finish the tunnel, it created a giant crater. But even with the tunnel ruined, Grant still sent soldiers in. So Grant decided to send black soldiers into this crater, but once in the crater the soldiers couldn't climb out the other side and were trapped. Seeing their chance, the Confederate soldiers rushed to the edge of the crater and shot the men to their death. But if these brave soldiers had been white men, the Confederates would have taken them captive instead. This is the first time I really realized how cruel war could be.

Nothing bad has happened in about a week so I hope this good luck streak continues. "Shhh." Someone hissed at us all. "There's someone hiding in the bushes up ahead." We all looked, and there was a man hiding there. He didn't look dangerous though. He seemed to be tarred and feathered, and had a look that told us he was fearing greatly for some thing.

"Hello out there!" one of our men called to him. "We come in peace." Slowly the distressed man came out of the bushes.

"Hello" he said. "I am a teacher who has been tarred and feathered for my willingness to help slaves to read and write. If you could do me the kind favor of protecting me until I find another place to hide I would be most grateful." This little man had just answered everyone's questions plus answered our offer to help him, and we barely had said a word to him.

"Of course we'll help you!" All of us agreed. But as we found out later, our kind act had delayed us a day. So that night after setting up camp we settled down for the news from Claire's letters. It was from a woman this time and her name was Cecilia. She said that the war's end encouraged her, but she continues to worry about the welfare of black citizens. She said how the President had resisted releasing the Emancipation Proclamation at the beginning of the war, to make a point that this war was not to abolish slavery but to keep the Union together. She says that without Mr. Douglass urging the president, he might have waited even longer. Cecilia also believes that even though Mr. Lincoln does not like slavery, he does not consider black people a white person's equal.

We are very close to being done with our journey. But we have had a great loss. Abraham Lincoln was assassinated several days ago, by John Wilkes Booth. We just have to travel about three or four more days and we should be at our destination in the North. Our group stopped to rest near a train station and while at our rest place we met a woman. She said that she was an abolitionist and she worked for women's rights. After we talked with her for some time, she offered us a way to cut our journey by about three days.

"If you answer this riddle, with one guess on your side, I'll pay for everyone's train fare," she said. We all agreed to this. The riddle is this:

"Bigger than a 'Little Giant,' I hold malice toward none, and charity toward all. I am, perhaps, a 'great star/ Early dropped in the western sky in the night.'

"Who am I?"

We all gathered in a group to discuss our thoughts. "I think that it's the moon," Claire said.

"No, it's obviously the sun," the tall muscular woman argued.

"You both have marvelous ideas," Susan said, "but I don't think that either of them are correct."

"I think I know!" I said. "It's Abraham Lincoln! I mean it all fits. He's 'bigger than a little giant,' and he holds 'malice towards none.' He has 'charity for all.' Also, he's a 'great star'."

"I see now," a man nodded. "'Early dropped in the western sky' must mean when he died several days ago!"

"Abraham Lincoln is our final answer," Susan said to the woman.

"Very good!" the woman smiled "You're all so smart and so now I will pay for your fare."

On the train Claire read us her last letter. It was from her friend Alan. He, too, had been going to the North. The only difference was that he was a black soldier coming home from war. He said, and I agree, that he hopes that all black soldiers get the honor and recognition they deserve for fighting for the Union cause. He described in the letter his longing for the safe North grounds. He also tells of his hopes that one day there will no longer be segregation, and that white and black people can participate in social and political activities together.

I know that Alan's hopes will come true as I look out of the train window. Because this is a forever changing world, and I know that future generations will look back on this and learn from our mistakes. And make the world a better place.

SUMMARY ASSESSMENT OF CONTENT AND LITERACY LEARNING

The conventional approach to assessing a student's understanding of disciplinary content is to ask the student to *report* what he or she has learned. But we gave students a few options, and Kathryn chose to share a narrative of her experience. This narrative reveals not only her considerable skills at telling a story but also the concepts and information she has learned about a historical era. Although a work of fiction, the narrative accurately reports events: the destruction of plantations and the plantation system in the South, the transition to freedom and the resulting challenges for employment, the threats to those who attempt to advance the literacy skills of slaves, the slaughter of men in the crater during the siege of Petersburg, the influence of Frederick Douglass, the assassination of Abraham Lincoln, and the poetic homage by Walt Whitman.

Kathryn opens with a dream sequence that serves as a flashback to reveal the conditions and trauma of the protagonist's life before the journey home from Appomattox. She invents the device of a sympathetic abolitionist who delivers a bundle of letters, which the recipient shares at intervals as a way to entertain the weary travelers. Kathryn quotes passages from the letters from the simulation, and these and the series of travel challenges serve to structure the narrative.

Kathryn provides sufficient sensory detail ("it had been replaced by a large cotton field with many slaves pricking their hands on the sharp needles of the cotton plant") and extensive dialogue to help the reader imagine setting, events, and characters and to give a sense of immediacy to the story. She conveys to the reader the goal of the travelers and the obstacles that threatened their aspirations. While the lengthy story has a series of episodes, they blend into each other within the broader journey structure to make the entire composition cohesive.

We judge that with her story Kathryn reveals that she has a keen sense of the horror of people living enslaved. She cites some of the terror and destruction of war, including Sherman's march and the siege of Petersburg. Kathryn notes the discriminatory treatment of Black soldiers who served in the Union Army, and recounts their slaughter in the crater at Petersburg. She comments on Lincoln's hesitancy in issuing the Emancipation Proclamation and the role of Frederick Douglass in urging the president to act. She contrasts the economies of the North and South and speculates about the economic recovery and the persistence of political and cultural tensions that follow protracted war.

Taken together, the interactions within teams, the discussions about letters and travel challenges, and the written reflections reveal that the students learned a great deal about the Civil War and its lingering effects on the nation, especially for their first formal exposure to this period of U.S. history. The various forms of complex communication show that the students are able to negotiate problem solving with their teammates, argue for a course of action, evaluate and respond to opposing views, and write a coherent and elaborated written response about their experience. We also see the beginnings of students' understanding of basic political and economic problems that persist into their contemporary world. We think we are realistic when we imagine that the students who had experienced the sequence of simulations described in this book might feel emboldened to contribute to adult conversations about the issues that divide political parties and regions of the country and share their understandings about how a complex of social, cultural, and economic factors might conspire to lead to war.

Chapter 6 provides the details for following the Road from Appomattox simulation. We describe the procedures and variations and note what to expect. We also describe how students have responded during the process, revealing the practice with procedures that account in part for the quality of the writing that students like Eric and Kathryn produced.

The Road from Appomattox

The elaborated student writings that we shared in Chapter 5 are the products, in part, of the students' involvement with their peers in a simulation that asked them to imagine a post–Civil War journey from Appomattox, Virginia, to their homes at various destinations in the United States. We judge that the simulation is in part responsible for the quality of the students' writing, because we understand that the many experiences throughout the school year had prepared the learners to write logical and coherent arguments and unified and compelling narratives. In this chapter we share the materials and procedures for the Road from Appomattox simulation game and offer advice for its use and variations.

In some ways this is the simplest of the three simulations that we share in this book. The supposition is that the Civil War has ended and the many participants who find themselves far from home or from their intended home will trek the difficult path to their destinations. As with the classic video games *The Oregon Trail* and *The Amazon Trail*, the players move toward a goal, with many obstacles hampering their progress. McCann's "Bridger Trail" (1996) follows a similar motif in a pioneer simulation. Two elements of the game offer layers of complexity. First, students work in teams, with each team representing a different persona. As with any collaborative effort, the problem-solving process gets complicated as the team members have to negotiate decisions with one another and determine how they will act when there is dissent. The other element of richness is the many documents that students read and share. Essential to the game is that the participants read letters and "travel challenges," summarize the content of these texts for their classmates, and defend their decisions before the critics who might see a strategic advantage in influencing the players to change their minds.

Here is the basic premise of the simulation, as we would offer it to our students: The long bloody war has finally ended. General Robert E. Lee of Virginia has met at the home of Wilmer McLean to sign the papers of surrender with Union general Ulysses S. Grant. While most of the armed combat is over, much of the suffering continues. Also, the difficult work of repairing the damage caused by war must begin.

The Civil War (or War Between the States, as some regions of the country still label it) was a significant shock and test of American democracy. Over a century and a half after the war, citizens of the United States still think about the meaning and effect of the war, and wonder what would have happened if General Lee and the Army of Northern Virginia had successfully resisted General Grant. Your experience in looking back on the war—its causes and many gruesome details, follies, and triumphs—will reveal much about why people would battle fellow countrymen and how the effects of the war linger today.

PLAYING THE GAME

As with any classroom activity that involves small-group work, the teacher will want to think carefully about how to establish the teams. As we note in Chapter 4 (see the section "Forming the Families"), we value diversity in each group. We look to include in each group a student who can assume leadership. We look to include both boys and girls, the more outspoken and the more diffident, the taskmaster and the learner who needs encouragement. If our class includes English language learners, we team these students with classmates who can be supportive, especially in understanding the nuances of language and in unveiling the cultural assumptions embedded in the documents and the rules of the game.

For convenience in distributing the documents that are specific to individual teams and in keeping track of team progress, we have assigned color codes to the teams: red, green, yellow, purple, brown, and gray. We know, for example, that only the red team receives a specific set of letters that are unique to its group and that the green team receives a different set of letters. We assign each group a general identity, such as Union soldiers, freedmen traveling south, or supporters heading south (see number 2 below). When the students meet in their individual teams they invent the details of their identities, including their past before the war and their experience during the war. Since they are traveling together, they have to figure out their relationships to one another and their roles within the group both for the sake of the play of the game (e.g., spokesperson, reader) and their imagined roles in the simulation (e.g., members of a family, friends from the military, colleagues in the same occupation). These details become part of their narrative as they write in their journal and when they assume a persona for writing about the whole experience.

The instructions below outline the play of the game. At each stage in the journey, each team receives an envelope with two documents—a letter from a friend or loved one, and a travel challenge. The construction of the letters is key here. We have taken care to construct 30 letters that reveal key details about the war—the major campaigns, the impact on civilian life and the land, the economic effects, the major figures in politics and the military, the roles of women, the experience of Black soldiers and so on. There are rich sources of sample letters available from the Library of Congress. As we note later in the chapter, Ward, Burns, and Burns have reproduced many letters in *The Civil War* (1990), and diarists such as Mary Chesnut also can inspire facsimile letters.

We have also sorted the letters to match their intended audience as defined by group roles. We share some sample letters below, and we offer a list of topics that might be the areas of emphasis in the letters. We certainly want to expose students to the major military campaigns, but the topics also focus on economic conditions, regional distinctions, political figures, and social implications. While we can offer only a few sample letters here, we make the entire set available on a website that warehouses all of the materials of the simulation: literacyandhistoryinaction.com.

The Journey Home

You and your classmates will try to imagine what it would have been like to live in the United States in 1865, especially to live in the areas most directly affected by the war. If you were at Appomattox at the time that the war ended, you would be eager to return home to your own family and to familiar surroundings. *What would that journey home be like? What would the journey teach you about the effects of the war?*

Here is how we will go about playing the game, with the object for each team of survivors to reach home as soon as possible.

1. You will join with three or four of your classmates to form a team to head home together. Your team will *compete with other teams* to see who can *get the closest to home* within *20 days*.
2. There are six teams: (a) Union soldiers headed north, (b) Confederate soldiers headed south, (c) Union supporters (nurses, provisioners, reporters, clergy, etc.), (d) Confederate supporters (nurses, provisioners, reporters, clergy, etc.), (e) northern-bound freedmen, and (f) southern-bound freedmen.
3. At each of five stages in your journey, you and your team members will face a difficult decision. Your response to the challenge *could* affect your progress toward home.
4. At each stage of your journey, you will also receive a letter. Each letter will reveal a detail about the conditions at home while you were away. Like anyone who received a letter from home during this era, you will want to cherish and protect the document, because you will need to use information from the letter as you continue your journey and reflection.

5. At each stage of your journey, every member of the team will *write a diary entry* to record the events of your trip and to reflect on the difficulties connected with the war: (1) Describe the travel challenge you faced and how you arrived at your decision and (2) report the news from home and your reaction to that news.
6. After each team member has completed the current diary entry, a representative from the team will *report to the rest of the class* about what has happened to the team. In this way, each team will learn from one another and will be able to track each team's progress.
7. As you continue on the journey, you will *track your progress* in two ways: on a timeline at the front of the room, and on a map that you will keep in your team folder.
8. At the end of your journey, you will *write your own summary* of the significant events on the trip, and *your reflection on the overall effect* that the Civil War had on people, the land, and the hope for the future.

THE LETTERS ALONG THE WAY

An obvious key to the experience is that students receive a series of letters during their imaginary journey from Appomattox to home. Our students seem to have been willing to suspend disbelief and accept the idea that the letters would find their way to them along the road. Part of the fun is receiving a letter and a travel challenge in an envelope. The communication then seems both personal and usually surprising. Students also seem to appreciate that each letter is accompanied by a photograph of the author, as if a friend or loved one had sent it as a sentimental gesture. We have tapped into the Library of Congress's extensive collection of vintage photographs to use with the letters. In Appendix K we identify the Library of Congress site and other resources for examples of letters of the era and photographs from the Civil War era.

We have provided below a few sample letters, as well as a list of possible topics to include in letters. We trust that many teachers will enjoy trying their hand at constructing similar letters. In our experience, two factors influenced the construction of the letters that might reveal much about the Civil War and Reconstruction. First, the teacher would have to know much about the war—its causes; its destruction; its influences on industry, invention, warfare, medicine, and politics; its lasting divisiveness; its hope for a "second American Revolution." We are not scholars of this period of U.S. history, but we have read a lot to guide our thinking about the simulation as a key element in our instruction about the Civil War and Reconstruction. Some of our reading is listed with other resources in Appendix K. We have tried not to overemphasize the military history of the period. Instead, we wanted to expand students' thinking into related economic, social, cultural, and political issues. We have found that James McPherson's *Battle Cry of Freedom* (2003) is especially helpful and explores concepts well beyond the military history. Similarly, Doris Kearns Goodwin's *A Team of Rivals* (2006) offers insight into the personalities and politics of the era. For details about the military history, teachers can turn to Shelby Foote's three-volume *The Civil War: A Narrative* (1974) and Bruce Catton's three-volume *Centennial History of the Civil War* (1965).

We also recommend that a teacher look at diaries and letters of the time. Mary Chesnut's *A Diary from Dixie* (1980) is perhaps the most familiar personal account from a Southern perspective, but sources like Ward, Burns, and Burns's *The Civil War* (1990) contain many examples of letters and diary entries from both Northern and Southern perspectives. We have tried to imitate as much as possible the style of the letters of the time, and we have devoted a different font for each set so that each team of travelers gets a kind of personalized set of missives. As our examples show, we have typically ended the letters with a question for the team to ponder and to write a response to in a journal. We have seen that the cumulative effect of these questions and responses is rich elaboration that students infuse into their summative responses, as we show in Chapter 5.

Any teacher preparing for a simulation that places students in an imagined environment of a historical era will obviously want to research that era. Throughout this book we have identified sources that have informed our thinking and enriched our planning. We have enjoyed the benefit of collaborating with the school librarian to prepare materials and to support students' research. We recommend that teachers encourage similar partnerships and rely on the librarians' assistance in finding the materials that will support teachers and students.

We offer sample letters for the simulation, but some teachers might want to try their hands at producing their own letters and recognize that no one can produce such an exhaustive collection of letters that they reveal the Civil War in all of its devastating and gory detail. We suggest that embedded in the letters, a teacher will want to expose students to some of the momentous events of the war, some noteworthy place names, and some of the key political and military figures. Here are a few events to consider: the attack on Harper's Ferry, the Fugitive Slave Law, the attack on Fort Sumter, the blockade of the South, the Emancipation Proclamation, conscription, the draft riots, the encounter between the *Monitor* and *Merrimac*, General Sherman's March to the Sea, and African Americans' entrance into combat. Key battles and noteworthy places include the First Battle of Bull Run/Manassas, the Siege of Vicksburg, the Battle of Shiloh, Antietam, Fredericksburg, Gettysburg, Andersonville, and the Siege of Petersburg. We judge that key figures would include Abraham Lincoln, Frederick Douglass,

Jefferson Davis, John Brown, Dred Scott, Clara Barton, Dorothea Dix, General Winfield Scott, General Grant, General Lee, General Sherman, General McClellan, and Andrew Johnson.

SAMPLE LETTERS

Dear Friend,

I hope that this letter finds you safe and in good health. I haven't written in weeks, because I, along with my fellow black soldiers, have been involved in the Siege of Petersburg.

If nothing else, General Grant is stubborn and persistent in his pursuit of the enemy. He doggedly pursued General Lee and his army from Richmond to Petersburg. Each time the two armies reached a stalemate, General Grant tried to outflank Lee's army by moving troops south to contain the Confederates' movement. But each time, Lee anticipated the maneuver and sent his army farther south until they stopped for one last defense at Petersburg. The Union Army had the Confederates contained, but found it impossible to overwhelm them. General Grant attempted almost every conceivable plan to break through the Southern defenses.

A group of soldiers, former coal miners from Pennsylvania, proposed to dig a tunnel right under the Confederate lines. Then they would load the tunnel with dynamite to blast an opening in the defenses. The tunneling took weeks. When the dynamite was set for blasting, a unit of black soldiers was prepared to rush through the area of the blast and enter through the Confederate fortifications. The blast made a huge crater in the earth. The black soldiers rushed in, but the hole was so deep that they could not easily ascend on the Confederate side. The rebel soldiers then stood at the rim of the crater and shot the soldiers to death, not taking any prisoners as they might have done if they had been white soldiers.

I can only hope that after the wounds of this war heal, all citizens, black and white, can live together in a spirit of brotherhood and unity. Do you think it will ever be possible?

Your friend,
Thaddeus

Dear Old Friend,

I know that you are returning home as I am. I wish you a safe trip. I am afraid of what we might find when we return home.

I expect that many of our old friends will be gone, because they were lost to wounds or disease during the long war. Their widows and children will need much help and emotional support to endure the dark years that lie before them. I don't know what we will do to earn a living. The businesses that once thrived in our town will be gone, and no one has money at the moment to invest in new businesses. I suppose that farming is always available to us, but one needs to own land to farm. The situation seems quite hopeless for us and for hundreds of thousands of others in the South. We will need the support of the government in Washington, DC, to survive these terrible times. During the war, our attention turned to our own survival; now we must think also of the survival of our families and our neighbors. How do you think Southerners will survive the coming years? Is it likely that the leaders in the North will help us in some way?

Your friend,
Jethro

Dear Son,

We are so proud of you for serving your country during time of war. After Gettysburg, when the president needed more soldiers, he instituted a draft, which meant that adult males could be selected to serve in the military, whether they wished to or not.

It would appear that the draft is the most democratic way to form an army, but that is true if we follow a consistent practice. The army actually allowed men to pay a sum of money to be excused from the draft. I have heard stories of men who have paid off other men to appear for military service in their place. In fact, I have heard that some men have accepted money from several men and appeared for military induction again and again, at several locations.

As you can imagine, there has been resistance to the draft in some cities. In fact, in New York City, there have been horrible draft riots, led mostly by immigrants who did not support the war and saw the newly liberated slaves as competition for jobs. I understand that dozens of people were killed in these riots. What do you think of such resistance to military service?

Sincerely,
Father

TRAVEL CHALLENGES

While the letters reveal details about the war and its possible aftermath, we also confront the teams with a series of travel challenges. As we demonstrate in this chapter, these challenges present the teams with some ethical dilemmas, value conflicts, and logistical difficulties. Again, the team members deliberate among themselves to determine a course of action. A spokesperson for each team shares the challenge and the decision with the rest of the class. This serves in part as a means of keeping everyone honest about reported progress in the journey, but it also subjects the decision and the rationale behind it to the scrutiny of the rest of the class. We offer a couple of sample challenges below, followed by a longer list of possibilities. Again, a teacher, especially in collaboration with colleagues, might want to turn a creative hand to constructing other travel challenges.

Travel Challenge 1: You come across a former soldier from the same army that you served. He has lost both legs to amputation as a result of injuries sustained during battle. He had been traveling on an old horse, but the horse has died, leaving the veteran soldier with no means for continuing his journey. If you take him to the nearest community, you will be delayed by 1 day. As you consider the problem, keep the following in mind:

- This former soldier was dedicated to supporting your cause and was willing to sacrifice his life in battle. His sacrifice calls for others to protect his dignity and honor.
- Without assistance, the former soldier will languish in the heat and dirt, trying as best he can to travel without aid.
- There is always the chance that other, more sympathetic travelers might come along the same route and offer assistance to the former soldier.
- The soldier was not an officer, and only officers were left with horses after the surrender. You have to wonder if this soldier came by his horse honestly.

If you provide aid to this former soldier, you will be delayed by *1 day*. What will you do?

Travel Challenge 2: An elderly couple emerge from the ruins of their home, destroyed by fire in the recent battles around Petersburg. They need to find new shelter but are too frail to travel without assistance. If you help, your assistance will delay you 1 day. As you discuss the problem, keep the following considerations in mind:

- The couple, residents of Virginia, were probably sympathetic to the Southern cause and would have supported the continued enslavement of human beings and the separation from the United States.
- The couple are elderly, and enfeebled as a result of lack of regular food and from the stress of war, especially over the past 10 months. It is unlikely that they can cause you any harm.
- The couple might remind you of your own grandparents.
- The couple could possibly struggle on their own to find new shelter, but they will be at serious risk of further harm if they are not able to find decent shelter by nightfall.

Your assistance to this elderly couple will cause you to be delayed by *1 day*. What will you do?

The two examples above offer a model for structuring a challenge with a current problem, its complicating details, and the protocol for the team's discussion. We list other possible challenges in Appendix I.

WORKING WITH NEW VOCABULARY

In Chapter 3, we suggested ways to introduce students to the content- and task-specific academic language embedded in the simulation about Colonial Elmtown. As the letters and travel challenges above reveal, the Road from Appomattox simulation also introduces vocabulary that is new to many of our students. Here, instead of previewing a rich array of language from the letters, we prefer to tackle new vocabulary as it comes along, because some of the vocabulary is specific to the context and would not be a natural part of our daily classroom interchanges. In addition, the new vocabulary is extensive and for most students we would simply be introducing them to it. We hope that many students internalize some of the new vocabulary, but we are mainly concerned that students grasp the gist of the letters. While our letters imitate to a certain extent the rhetoric of the 19th century and sometimes use vocabulary that is both quaintly antiquated and foreign to our students, we tackle this new language together, group by group and document by document. We advise, however, that a teacher introduce early the language of the writing prompts. This is the abstract academic language that directs students in completing their compositions. Here is a brief scan of the kind of academic language students need to know: *explain in a report, draw from journals, provide specific details, describe the effects, appeal to the president, recommend a course of action, write a narrative in five episodes* (i.e., the five stages of the game), *establish a central conflict, create vivid and realistic characters, sequence events, include dialogue.* This is obviously not an exhaustive list, but it itemizes some abstract language that seems common in school but might be nebulous for the some younger writers or for students who have made a relatively recent transition from an English as a Second Language or sheltered English program.

COMPLICATING ELEMENTS: RANDOM PROBLEMS

As we developed the simulation, we recognized that besides experiencing the orchestrated travel challenges, each team would be subject to chance occurrences. During any journey, events that are beyond the control of the travelers sometimes befall them. The apparently random events are unanticipated and defy the travelers' ability to plan or to make strategic decisions, and these events call for a collective response to enable survival and for the journey to continue.

Given the random events that follow, this feature of the journey will delay all the travelers. One could easily add to the variety of situations, and some of them could be benefits that advance the progress of the travelers (e.g., they discover a shortcut), while other situations present obstructions (e.g., a forest fire triggered by heat lightning forces a circuitous passage). In the interest of keeping the game competitive and adhering to time constraints, teachers can limit the events to negative situations only, or a mixture of benefits and delays.

A simple random means for assigning events to each group is to have a representative roll dice or choose a corresponding number from a jar. We list some random problems in Appendix J.

RESOURCES TO SUPPORT DEVELOPMENT OF SIMULATION MATERIALS

Earlier in this chapter we identified for teachers some common texts that provide detailed narratives of the Civil War, its causes, and its consequences, and we list these titles in Appendix K. We have also tapped into several on-line resources for examples of primary source texts and photographs to help teachers to build the simulation. As we note in detail in Chapter 7, while the simulation is a kind of game, it is also a shared inquiry process, with students joined together in connecting events, speculating about causes, and reflecting on effects. A central problem drives the inquiry as students attempt to understand why states that made up one union would engage in a long and bitter war against one another and to identify the lasting consequences of that war. But investigators need access to information in order to advance their inquiry. We have found several web resources very useful for images, documents, narratives, and other information that help us to construct the material in the simulation. We list these sites in Appendix K. These sites also serve students whose interest we pique and who want to read further about this era of our history.

JOURNAL WRITING AND FORMATIVE ASSESSMENT

In Chapter 5, we offer the journal prompt that guides students in writing about their simulated experiences. The journal writing serves the important function of structuring the means for learners to record revelations about major events in the war, the personal tribulations and dilemmas that each team faced, and understandings of the impact and consequences of the war. After each stage in the journey, we ask students to write in their journals so they have an immediate record of experience. As students write, we move from learner to learner to see what they have recorded and perhaps prompt them to elaborate further about the immediate events and their meaning. This check on the journal informs us about the students' insights and areas of confusion. As with the other simulations, this one would be organic, with teachers adding elements and reviewing events as needed. The journal also serves as a means to collect information and recollections from which to draw in order to write the summative response to the experience. Here are some recurring questions that prompt journal entries:

- What have you learned about the suffering and destruction that have resulted from the war?
- What difficulties have you and your companions faced on your journey home?
- How did you and your companions resolve the difficulties or solve the problems that confronted you? Explain why you made the decisions you made, and describe the process you followed to make your decisions.
- What difficulties did other teams face, and how did they resolve problems and make decisions?

EXTENDING AND EXPANDING THE INQUIRY

As with the other simulations, our students have found ways to extend and expand their learning. We have sometimes found a common text to share with an entire class, but we have also identified related titles and encouraged students to pursue their interests in learning more about the war and its aftermath. We have listed some of these titles in Appendix K. This is a limited bibliography, and a teacher's work with the school librarian will help in expanding this list of possibilities or in creating similar lists for other topics.

Sometimes students become engrossed in specific aspects of the war and the era—the use of submarines, the emergence of ironclads, the reliance on spies, the women who served in combat or as spies, or military heroes and specific battles. We encourage these enthusiasms and find ways for individual students to share what they have discovered.

We judge also that students' inquiry into the rivalries that prompted war, the cultural and economic distinctions across the nation, the abhorrence of slavery and the stubborn protection of it, and the assessment of President Lincoln as a political and moral leader has positioned them to think about issues in their contemporary world—why there might be "red states" and "blue states," how political expediency might win over moral rectitude, how heroes surrender their personal comfort and safety for the advancement of a cause, how war demonstrates the lowest of human folly and reveals the most admirable human qualities, and so on. In the end, students come to a stronger understanding of where the country has come from and why rifts and rivalries remain in a united nation. We can well imagine students' processing the conversations around the dinner table through the lens of their experience as Civil War–era travelers.

CHAPTER 7

Framing Inquiry in Action

The instructional material that we share in this book is not offered as a curriculum guide; we recognize that specific instructional contexts and goals will require adapting the activities to work well with a specific group of learners. We are more concerned with illustrating how such discussion-based inquiry activities work—how real students react to them, how they learn content knowledge, and how they produce elaborated written responses. Individual teachers might emphasize other discipline-specific content, such as the Great Depression, the framing of the Constitution, exploration and discovery, forming colonies, and entering and surviving world wars. If this book has any value as a tool for classroom teachers, it will reveal possible structures and procedures for other simulations to involve learners actively in the experiences under study in a school. We hope that we have demonstrated ways for history to come alive while students remain active in purpose-driven literacy, including talking, listening, reading, researching, and writing.

We offer here some guidelines and considerations for constructing simulation games and simulation role-playing activities or adapting ours. Troyka and Nudelman (1975) offer useful models for the design of simulations, and Gee (2007) describes elements of a design grammar for producing highly engaging video games. We draw inspiration and principles from these two sources to design instruction that we hope leads to the kind of "authentic pedagogy" that Newmann and colleagues (1996) outline.

BASIC PRINCIPLES

As we have designed interactive and inquiry-based instructional activities, we have remained true to two basic principles: (1) The activity must focus on a problem that students care about and (2) the activity must give students substantial opportunity to interact with one another. The principles are likely to strike any teacher as simple and obvious, but honoring these principles requires both attention to detail and the discipline to stay true to the inquiry process, especially when the teacher feels compelled to *explain things* and *transmit* a body of knowledge.

If the activity represents a line of *inquiry*, then a problem must drive the effort. This emphasis on problems and problem solving invites a close examination of the nature of problems and their importance in driving inquiry and learning. While we can acknowledge that every student will have a primary or preferred learning modality (Gardner, 2011; Smagorinsky, 1991), we agree with Willingham that our learners have more in common than in contrast and are essentially problem solvers: "Thinking is slow and unreliable. Nevertheless, people enjoy mental work if it is successful. People like to solve problems, but not to work on unsolvable problems" (2009, p. 3). From this perspective, learners might not all enjoy "brain teasers" and conundrums but will enjoy tackling what they see as everyday sort of problems, especially if they see the problems as relevant, realistic, and significant enough to invest some effort in solving. Given the examples that we have showcased in this book, a reader might wonder how a legislative hearing, a series of town hall meetings, and an imagined journey from Appomattox to some fictional destination represent compelling problems for 5th-graders or for students in middle school or high school. We suggest that the problems boil down to issues that resonate with preadolescent and adolescent learners: How can we treat people fairly? What is the appropriate way to respond to offenders who have done great harm to others? What are the limits of our freedom? Must we always obey authority? How long will we endure impingements on our freedom before we resist and protest? How do we advance and protect the common good? What are my individual obligations to contribute to the common good? How much am I willing to sacrifice to protect principles and to help people who are less fortunate? While these questions have broad policy implications for a nation, students recognize that they also apply to daily events in the classroom and local community. So we begin with these meaningful problems and design an inquiry sequence and the structures for deliberation around the problems.

A GUIDE TO CONSTRUCTING SIMULATIONS
AND OTHER INQUIRY ACTIVITIES

We have long been suspicious of claims about "best practice." While we ascribe to the principle that sound theory and a firm research foundation should drive classroom practice, we recognize that theory and research often describe general trends and do not account for all teachers and all learners in all situations. We offer here the basic structure and some important details that we keep in mind when we design the kind of activities that we share in this book. This is not a foolproof recipe. Just as the recommended directions from the map app on a smartphone might encourage the user to pay attention to actual live traffic conditions, we advise that the user of these directions know a particular group of students well and adapt the focus and the activity structures to meet the learners' specific needs and interests. Given this caution, we proceed with the thinking that for us drives the construction of learning activities that immerse students in thinking about history and communicating in complex ways.

1. Problems: Frame a problem that resonates with the specific group of learners. The broad problem (e.g., Who has the right to rule? How can we repair systematic damage to a group of people? What is the balance between individual rights and social responsibility?) will represent essential questions associated with a discipline like social studies and will provide the overall structure for the line of inquiry. Within the broad problem there will be a series of ancillary problems. For example, within the Colonial Elmtown simulation, the students had to contend not only with broad political issues like the garrisoning of soldiers within their community but also with other problems as significant as guarding against spies in their midst and as mundane as addressing an epidemic of milk sickness and a rash of petty crimes. The ancillary or less significant problems represent some of the obstacles standing in the path of solving the broad, overarching problem, which is quite similar to current endeavors for solving broad, overarching problems in the world today (sending aid to starving people in war-torn regions), when conditions (corruption among local powers, unwelcoming terrain, cultural predispositions) seem to conspire against the delivery of help.

2. Goals for the "Game": As with any well-designed video game, the simulation must establish a clear goal for the participants: pass a bill, reach consensus regarding a response to oppression, reach home before others, and so on. The goal drives the action of the participants and provides the mark for measuring progress and accomplishment. Gee (2007) and Smith and Wilhelm (2006) note that two elements make video games especially appealing to players: They always know the goal they are trying to reach (attain a level, destroy enemy attackers, travel safely) and have a distinct sense of their current status in realizing the goal. As Smith and Wilhelm (2006) point out, this dynamic combination of goal awareness and recurring assessment is part of a *flow experience*, as defined by Csikszentmihalyi (1990).

3. Goals for Learning: Identify specific learning outcomes. The expression of these outcomes is likely to be influenced by specific discipline standards (e.g., NCTE, ILA, or NCSS), as well as social and emotional learning standards. The effort to meet the goals of the game allowed students to work toward specific learning targets. Part of the process of designing the simulation involves envisioning the kind of performance that the teacher can expect from the learners at the end of the process and then planning backward for the experiences that appear logically to prepare all learners to achieve the targets. In the examples we offer in this book, we expected some complicated thinking and complex communication: Define an abstract concept (*reparations*) by expressing essential criteria illustrated by specific examples, collect data through personal research and the shared inquiry of the class to make informed judgments about policy (*deliberative argument*), apply criteria in judging the appropriateness and form of reparations (*epideictic argument*) in a letter to a principal and to a legislator, express in discussion and writing the causes that led to specific historical events and political and economic conditions (*forensic argument*). In order to accomplish the tasks listed above, students would have to command substantial knowledge about Native Americans and their cultural clashes with non-Native settlers, about the events that preceded armed conflict in the American Revolutionary War, and about the result of prolonged hostilities during the Civil War. In addition, we had in mind how students would proceed during deliberations and teamwork. We expected students to follow appropriate protocols for problem solving as a small team and for deliberating as a larger body of thinkers. Rubrics can help in defining learning targets and serve to measure performance and development. In many ways, it is hard to separate assessment from goals, because our provisions for assessing performance forces us to define in detail what we hope to see in performance. Many of the goals focus on *procedures—researching, discussing, judging, responding, deferring, paraphrasing, arguing*, and so on—and we have found ourselves assessing learners through close observation in the moment when *students are in action*. Some goals do not lend themselves to objective measure and quantification: for example, that students have listened closely to the contributions of their peers and assessed fairly the merits of competing points of view. In other words, we seek evidence that students are demonstrating how responsible citizens operate civilly and rationally in a democratic society, by listening to them and observing their actions, not by grading paper-and-pencil exams.

4. Access to Information: Of course, problem solving requires access to information. In the design of the simulation, the teacher would either provide data sets or build in a stage for students to access information themselves, or both. In the examples in this book, we describe a simulation in which the information comes largely through the documents we provide the students. In working with 5th-graders, we found it most sensible to provide students texts; with older students we might build in a stage to help students find related documents. In the case of the Road from Appomattox simulation, students could rely on 30 letters and various travel challenges to reveal events of the war and the experience of the populations affected by the war and the conditions that preceded it. In the legislative hearing about a reparations bill, teams of students researched individual tribes and shared their findings in public testimony at our simulated hearing. For Colonial Elmtown, we provided information through our introduction of the crisis of the day and through various primary source documents. In addition, students sought information on their own, as they attempted to understand the change in the value of currency over time and tried to sort out the conflicting reports about what really happened in the Boston "massacre."

5. Teams, Roles, Identity, and Points of View: All the simulations that we describe involve students in formulating arguments and assessing the arguments of others. We judge that the conditions are right for learning when students experience some sense of doubt. We raise doubts by introducing debatable problems, but also by establishing competing points of view, which is essential to debate. The recognition and disposition of alternative points of view is part of logical thinking and emphasized in the Common Core State Standards as essential to argument. Toulmin (2000) notes that fully developed arguments include evaluation of a rebuttal position. Not only do we want to introduce a variety of perspectives, but we also build in protocols that require discussion participants to introduce their comments by first paraphrasing and responding to the previous speaker. This is most obvious during the town hall meetings in Colonial Elmtown. In each simulation we have organized the class into small groups and assigned a general identity to each group, which may naturally give rise to a point of view about the various events and problems. The students then enjoy establishing the details of their family, group, and individual identity, even designing an emblem to represent themselves in any graphic display of game progress.

6. Rules of the Game: As with any game, the simulation requires rules. Without getting too complex, the rules guide the procedures and the accountability in each simulation. Knowing the rules is especially important when the game is competitive and the students want to check one another's accuracy in marking progress and staying true to the rules. Following the rules of the game requires some form of record-keeping to track progress. Journal writing serves as a form of record-keeping, as do the written reports that are necessary for movement from one phase to another. When the game involves competition, as with the Road from Appomattox, it is useful to have a visual display (e.g., timeline and map) in the room and the public reporting of decisions to reveal positions. When the simulation occurs over several days, the journal writing allows students to keep a record of whether each group advances or is delayed, based on the choices they have made and the calamities that may have befallen them.

7. Forums and Decorum: For us, discussion is essential to the proceedings. We urge anyone designing a simulation to build in several opportunities for students to talk to one another. These opportunities involve small-group work (e.g., team preparation, "family" discussions), large-group discussions (the debriefings in each simulation), and fishbowl formats (e.g., the town hall meetings). We judge that the interaction among peers is essential to understanding and problem solving. The dynamics of exploring and evaluating options, challenging positions, responding to challenges, recognizing alternatives, paraphrasing, and clarifying conclusions are all part of argument and critical thinking. Through their frequent interactions, students immerse themselves in the procedures that are necessary for decisionmaking and for writing compositions in a variety of modes—telling their story, arguing for a policy, or reporting events (McCann, 2014). We recommend that a teacher who designs a simulation include specific discussion structures that seem logically connected to the simulated environment: committee work, legislative hearings, family meetings, town hall meetings, and so on. We have found that students are both willing and enthusiastic about assuming a new identity and playing a role during the forums that require peer interaction during the simulation.

8. Integrated Literacy: We want our students to have a sense of play as they are learning, but much of the learning involves literacy experiences, including speaking and listening. Throughout the simulation and in the end, we expect students to read and write a lot. The writing includes journal entries, research reports, collaborative responses, letters, pamphlets, broadsides, stories, news reports, and reflections. The reading includes online and print research, the examination of primary source documents, the sharing of letters from family and friends, reference to textbooks, and immersion in historical fiction. In the context of the simulation, students experience these literacy events as a natural and necessary part of the game and not as an assignment or onerous task. We have relied on the various forms of writing, and especially the summative writing, as essential assessments of students' learning, both of the proficiencies of writing, reading, and research and of the deep understanding of social studies content and concepts.

9. Autonomy and Self-Expression: While we have carefully orchestrated the simulations that we share in this book, we have built in opportunities for student choice and self-expression. For example, we have formed teams as "families" for Colonial Elmtown, but students have invented their family history, the relationships between the members of the family, and the emblem that would represent them as a unit. They also chose who would be the family spokesperson at a town hall meeting and the rotation of speakers for their family. We did require the each family member take a turn in representing the family, allowing for experiences related to the Common Core Standards for speaking and listening. Individual teams volunteered to write consensus reports (letters or pamphlets that expressed the sentiments or decisions of the town), and students chose the mode of writing for their summative response to the experience. In addition, and often to our surprise, students researched topics and produced artifacts that we never thought of assigning. As we report in Chapter 3, students produced political cartoons, physical mock-ups of homes and shops, newspapers, maps, and floor plans. Students also researched topics that piqued their interest, including the value of currency and of selected commodities, compared with modern prices, and even the re-creation of a lacrosse tournament during Colonial times. Some students became intrigued by the role of spies and the ingenious ways to communicate clandestinely and in code. These individual expressions add dimension to the simulation and make the imagined environment more "real." Although a teacher cannot exactly plan for these serendipitous inspirations, she can certainly allow the opportunities and encourage the efforts.

10. Extensions and Expansions: We designed the goals, rules, and procedures for each simulation as a rich experience in itself, but we also saw a need to connect the study to other elements in the curriculum so that the simulation was not a digression but a fully integrated element in the broader plan for learning. An obvious extension would be the reading of related historical fiction, either as shared reading, literary circles, or individual pursuits. For each simulation we have identified some related titles (see Appendix K). When students learn procedures for research, argument, or team problem solving, it is useful to introduce new opportunities to practice and refine these procedures. In addition, and perhaps most important, we want to connect the events of the past to contemporary events and debates. If we consider reparations for the harms experienced by Native Americans, shouldn't we apply the same principles in deciding reparations for Japanese Americans and African Americans? Looking beyond our borders, how would we decide the issue of reparations for victims of the Holocaust or of the attempts at genocide in Armenia, Rwanda, or Darfur? All the simulations prompt a reflection on our responsibilities to other members of our communities, the extent and limitations of our liberties, and the price we are willing to pay to protect ourselves and our neighbors. Less significant, but always with us, is the question of the role of government and taxes and how we define our political principles, vexing problems that we can link to Colonial times and to the hotly contested issues that led to civil war. If students can apply the thinking to contemporary issues and move into adulthood with a sense of how people can disagree but still deliberate about actions that are just and serve the common good, then the simulations are more than temporary diversions or amusements.

11. Assessment: If the simulation is a tool for learning, then it makes sense to build in assessments to judge what students have learned and how they have progressed over time. We have relied on written responses as summative assessments, and we have collected baseline writing samples as bases for comparison. In addition to this broad measure of learning, we rely on journal writing and the daily interactions within small groups and in the large-group forums to reveal proficiencies at communication and collaboration. Of course, careful observations during simulations support the assessment of students' progress. But this requires that a teacher have an awareness of each discussion forum and each phase in a sequence of activities. If the discussions about scenarios are intended to help students express criteria for judging the appropriateness and form for reparations, then a teacher will listen for these rules and help students to summarize and record them. Of course, the students' responses will let the teacher know if it is time to go forward or to extend or alter the discussion to accomplish the desired end.

   12. Reflection: This entire book is a reflection on practice, and we hope that we have also reflected on action. But we also want students to reflect on their experience. We have asked students in discussing and writing to explain how they were able to do what they did and what they think they have learned. One function of these reflections is to foster an awareness of procedures so that there is an increased likelihood that students can repeat the same processes (e.g., writing, researching) when they have other opportunities. We also want to know if the students found the activities engaging. We have an obligation to study the content and concepts that the school district sets as priorities, and we make our best judgments about what specific disciplines to elevate as essential. We take into account the expectations of the community and the values of our society at large. But we also want to take into account what interests our students and the conditions of learning that keep them engaged.

   It is also important to keep in mind that our simulations have developed organically. Each time we engage the learners in a simulation, we discover new possibilities. For example, the introduction of random problems was an addition to Colonial Elmtown, as was the History Sleuth. We also recognized over time that students needed to know more about the instability and irregularity of currency in Colonial America in order to appreciate the value of land as a stable asset and to judge the impact of taxes. We have not shared every possible variation, and we trust that reflective teachers will adapt to their teaching context and the needs and interests of their learners. In a sense, then, the simulation is never finished. This potential for growth and revision is an exciting element, keeping us looking forward to the next opportunity when we can add a new dimension and refresh the game.

THE DIALOGIC SPIRIT OF THE SIMULATION

We describe above some basic principles for developing curriculum. For the most part, these are the principles outlined long ago by Ralph Tyler—drawing on studies of learners, the discipline, and the society to inform what to teach.

But Tyler (1969) also advises that we subject these studies to two filters: the filter of our understanding of how humans learn, and the filter of our philosophical values. *In our case, we judge that learners learn best when they are actively engaged in experiencing (at least in a simulated way) what others have experienced during real historical dramas.* The action involves plenty of interaction, allowing students to practice various procedures and to construct understandings of event, concepts, and principles.

We also value the idea that students can learn to deliberate about questions of some consequence: How much do we value our freedom? How do we repair damage done to others? How do we treat everyone justly? Must we obey authority? How do we treat vanquished foes? We value the idea that discussants will disagree, but we expect them to disagree in a constructive way that still protects the dignity of an apparent adversary and allows merit where merit exists. Indeed, we judge that a dialogic classroom is a democratic classroom, in the sense of one that is inclusive and fosters respect for the diversity of thought.

THE EFFECT OF SIMULATIONS

Throughout this book we have shared students' writing to demonstrate what students have learned about history and to showcase their proficiencies at written expression, supported in large part by their reading of a range of texts and by their participation in various conversations with peers. We have not designed an experimental treatment study in which we could compare the growth of the students who have participated in the simulations with a control group that followed some alternative activities. Our only basis for comparison is the contrast with previous years when we taught history in a more conventional way. Each time we have read the summative writing from our students we have been impressed with the quality of their thinking, the elaboration of their expression, and the care they have taken in constructing complex texts. For a long time, we have worked with students of approximately the same age as the students who participated in the simulations. If there is any control group, it is the presimulation students; we can say with confidence that we have seen far more mature and elaborated writing from the students who have participated in the simulations than similar learners who came before them. We judge that our students have learned a lot. We have taken care to collect baseline measures of their writing and reading to track progress over the course of the year, but we have also relied a great deal on daily observations to assess other skills and habits of thinking.

Consistently, we have seen that students have been able to write with appropriate diction and appeals to address a specific audience. In some instances, students have imitated the diction of the time period when the characters they represented would have lived. We have seen that students command the rudiments of logical thinking—making claims supported by relevant information (examples, statistical data, testimonies) and interpreted with the established warrants. Students typically recognize and evaluate competing points of view. Some writing (e.g., History Sleuth) required the examination of contrasting accounts of the events of history, and students demonstrated that they were able to draw from their knowledge of history, cultivated through their "lived" experience, to evaluate the two accounts of events in order to explain the relative merits of the two views, requiring both synthesis and critical judgment. We have seen from the writing across the school year that students were able to command important elements of narrative writing—conveying a central conflict; establishing characters; proceeding through a logical sequence of related events and reactions; describing setting, characters, and events in sufficient detail; and handling dialogue in a realistic and precise way.

The students' written work has also revealed to us that the learners were able to read informational texts and literary texts with recall and understanding. They obviously drew from their reading of print and on-line resources to produce the necessary reports for the legislative hearing (Chapters 1 and 2). They read a variety of primary source documents, the textbook, and images to draw conclusions about the events that led to the American Revolutionary War (Chapters 3 and 4) and to reflect on the impact of the Civil War (Chapters 5 and 6). We know that the participation in the simulated historical experiences launched students into a variety of related texts—some historical fiction and some informational texts, some shared as a class and some read as individual pursuits.

An essential element in each of the simulations is the interactions they elicit among peers. We understand that in many ways students learn to write by talking (Applebee & Langer, 2013; Hillocks, 1995, 1999; McCann, 2014; Smagorinsky et al., 2010). We judge further that the purposeful talk among students helps them to gain a deeper understanding of what they have read. But we also see that the talk—the speaking and listening—among peers has value in itself. We want students to be able to take on a debatable issue or policy question and talk about their disagreements or deliberate about an appropriate consensus response without ridicule, disrespect, or inaccurate portrayal of an opposing position. While we introduced doubt and controversy as the engines to drive inquiry and encourage discussions, we established protocols for deliberations. We have been impressed that students consistently lived by the rules of the game and conducted themselves in the simulated hearing, town hall meetings, and debriefings in ways that many deliberative bodies in the adult world would do well to imitate. We were impressed especially that our students could paraphrase the reports and positions of their classmates, evaluate these contributions reasonably, and connect to previous speakers (i.e., uptake) as a means for extending and contextualizing the conversation. While we have offered a rubric for evaluating speaking and listening (Appendix B), we know that the assessment of these proficiencies will be largely informal, but will be essential for the formative judgments that will guide how the activities progress.

Part of our assessment of the effect of simulations requires appreciation of students' unsolicited efforts, both from individuals and teams. In Chapter 3 we share some of these examples. Students have produced posters and political cartoons, broadsides and pamphlets, maps, floor plans, and models of homes and shops. In one instance, a student was determined to understand and share with his classmates the comparable prices of goods and commodities when 18th-century prices are projected into contemporary dollars. We know from parents that students involved mom or dad or siblings at home in acquiring the materials and completing independent projects. Sometimes friends worked together outside school to construct something that illustrated how colonists lived or how they might have reacted to feelings of oppression.

We have been especially pleased to see hopeful signs that students can draw from their thinking about historical crises to contribute to adult conversations today about perennial political and economic issues. We judge that many of our students can speak intelligently and reasonably about reparations, the necessity or oppression of taxes, the rights of states and the power of the federal government, and the appropriate processes for deliberations about difficult and potentially volatile issues.

The simulations foray into the same territory explored by mature scholars, requiring a command of a significant body of information and the procedures necessary to make critical judgments and convey analysis in complex ways. As we assert in our Introduction, we have proceeded with the simulations under the assumption that all students are gifted and need to be included in the processes. We see a marvelous effect when we affirm explicitly that everyone has the abilities necessary to contribute to the activity; in fact, the simulation cannot function without the contributions of everyone, and the more diverse the thinking and the more varied the perspectives, the better. All students have contributed, sometimes with the support of a teaching assistant and sometimes with attention to the individual student's particular strength. We wouldn't want any teacher to be discouraged by the complexity of any one of the simulations, because we have seen all students participate and thrive with these experiences.

STUDENTS' REFLECTIONS

Of course, we have been quite impressed with what we have judged students have learned during their experiences with simulations like Colonial

Elmtown—so impressed that we have written a whole book about it. But we turn now to the impressions of our students. From time to time we have asked students to reflect on their learning. We have prompted them to comment on how they were able to complete a particular writing task successfully and to reflect on the quality of their experience during an entire unit of study. These written reflections serve two purposes: (1) fostering an awareness that students have followed a specific process to compose or research or deliberate so that they can consciously invoke and perhaps adapt the same processes to accomplish similar tasks in new situations and (2) revealing if the students had a generally positive experience with activities that we judged to be highly engaging. These written reflections take little time, and we have relied on the format of a simple letter—either to the teacher or to future students in the same class. We admit that students might have written positive reflections in order to please their teachers, but we trust that they recognized our willingness to alter any one of the activities or to abandon it entirely if the students had a negative response.

Megan noted that the work with her peers helped her to understand a sequence of causes leading to the Revolutionary War: "Participating in Elmtown helped me understand better the different stages leading to the Revolutionary War because we got to talk together as a family. If you were confused by anything there was almost always someone who could understand it and help you." Brandon also reflects on the effect of the interactions with his team and the others in his class: "By using the textbook, I can't see their opinions so it is not as easy to understand the war. Talking in families helped me understand what was so bad about the stages. For example, I didn't know what made the Sugar Act so bad but talking in the meetings helped me realize what was bad about it."

In her reflections, Maggie emphasized that the activities were *fun* and that they gave her *insight* into the way events might foment revolt: "I enjoyed Elmtown very much. It was fun getting to act like the colonists. It was much more helpful to learn about the colonies during Elmtown than reading about it because reading in the textbook was very boring." She notes further that active participation allowed her to feel what colonists long ago must have felt: "Participating in Elmtown helped me understand how hard it really was for the colonists with all King George's laws. We felt the same way that many of the colonists felt. Everyone paid better attention while doing Elmtown because we weren't just reading about the colonists' memories, we were acting them out."

In a letter to Becky D'Angelo, Dylan sums up many of the reflections of his classmates. He also reveals an awareness of the processes he followed and what elements of the experience helped him with his writing and with his appreciation of what American colonists must have experienced under the rule of King George III and Parliament.

Dear Mrs. D'Angelo,

I did enjoy learning about colonial America and the stages leading to the American Revolution through the Elmtown experience. This is because doing an interactive learning project like this allows you to be in the shoes of the people who were involved in the history you are studying. It gives you practice in debating civilly.

Participating in Elmtown helped me to understand the problems that led to the American Revolutionary war because when you play the part of the colonists you understand how they felt and how bad it got. Talking with my family and at town meetings helped me because it is a simulation of the real thing. That makes it feel as if you are the colonists and share information with peers, which is one of the best ways for students to learn.

I used the information from my family discussions and the town meeting to help me write the final essay because that allowed me to sum up the information and record it in a way that would be easy to gain information from. That way it is easy to get the information for the writing project.

I would give newbies this advice: Do the journals right after you get the information because it is fresh in your mind and if you need more information go to reliable websites.

Dylan Mahoney

FINAL THOUGHTS

As students move on to middle school or high school, they sometimes return to tell us about their experience. We have heard repeatedly from the students themselves and from our colleagues at these other schools in our district that our students feel that they have a bit of an advantage in knowing about Native American culture and experience, about Colonial times, and about the Civil War and Reconstruction. We judge from these unsolicited testimonies that their involvement in the simulations has helped students to develop a deep knowledge base on which they can study history again in middle school and high school.

We could not help but notice students' enthusiasm about being part of the simulations. When Tom checks in at the school office during his visits to facilitate town hall meetings or other forums, the secretary and the school nurse report that the students have been eagerly expecting him—not because of his vibrant personality, but because his visit means that the students will immerse themselves in some imagined period of history. Colonial Elmtown, which we have used the most frequently, has become a kind of legacy. Older siblings tell their brothers or sisters that this is a distinctive part of 5th grade, and something to look forward to. Students ask from the beginning of the year when they will begin Elmtown.

In designing all the activities that we share in this book, we have been concerned that students learn a lot about history, about reading, and about writing; we think we have planned carefully with attention to students' access to accurate information about history and with consideration to alignment to principles of learning. In planning together, we have also been adamant that students *enjoy* their experience. This does not mean that we pander to young people and strive to orchestrate their amusement. Instead, we plan activities in which all students feel equally competent to participate. We affirm that all students can learn what we set out to learn together. We emphasize their many competencies instead of underscoring their deficits. We allow students many opportunities to make decisions, and we remain flexible enough to adapt to the situation and the needs of the specific group of learners. We make sure that students have plenty of opportunities to talk to one another. We see these many conversations as necessary for learning important literacy procedures and critical thinking processes, as we have illustrated throughout the book. We also see the interactions among peers as necessary for forming a sense of community, which helps students to care about what they are doing and commit to finishing projects and meeting self-imposed responsibilities. In the end, the experiences of learning literacy skills and history *in action* help learners to be aware of how they have learned and involve students in procedures that they can apply in their learning at other grades and in their relationships with others in their homes and community, especially when everyone doesn't agree and important decisions must be made.

References

Applebee, A. N. (1986). Problems in process approaches: Toward a reconceptualization of process instruction. In A. R. Petrosky & D. Bartholomae (Eds.), *The teaching of writing: 85th yearbook of the National Society for the Study of Education* (pp. 95–113). Chicago, IL: University of Chicago Press.

Applebee, A. N., & Langer, J. A. (2013). *Writing instruction that works: Proven methods for middle and high school classrooms.* New York, NY: Teachers College Press.

Avi. (1984). *The fighting ground.* New York, NY: HarperCollins.

Bazerman, C., & Paradis, J. G. (Eds.). (1991). *Textual dynamics of the professions: Historical and contemporary studies of writing in professional communities.* Madison, WI: University of Wisconsin Press. Available at wac.colostate.edu/books/textual_dynamics/

Burke, J. (2010). *What's the big idea? Question-driven units to motivate reading, writing, and thinking.* Portsmouth, NH: Heinemann.

Charles, C. L., & Stadsklev, R. (1973). *Learning with games: An analysis of social studies educational games and simulations.* Boulder, CO: ERIC Clearinghouse for Social Studies.

Chesnut, M. (1981). *Mary Chesnut's Civil War.* New Haven, CT: Yale University Press.

Collier, J. L., & Collier, C. (1974). *My brother Sam is dead.* New York, NY: Macmillan.

Csikszentmihalyi, M. (1990). *Flow: The psychology of optimal experience.* New York, NY: HarperCollins.

Dewey, J. (1998). *Experience and education.* West Lafayette, IN: Kappa Delta Pi. (Original work published 1938)

Dewey, J. (2008). *Democracy and education.* Radford, VA: Wilder. (Original work published 1918)

Elkind, D. (2007). *The power of play: How spontaneous, imaginative activities lead to happier, healthier children.* Cambridge, MA: Da Capo Press.

Gardner, H. (2011). *Frames of mind: The theory of multiple intelligences.* Philadelphia, PA: Basic Books.

Garvey, D. M., & Garvey, S. K. (1967, December). Simulation, role-playing, and sociodrama in the social studies. *The Emporia State Research Studies, 16*(2), 5–34.

Gee, J. P. (2007). *What video games have to teach us about learning and literacy.* New York, NY: Palgrave Macmillan.

Graham, S., & Perin, D. (2007b). *Writing next: Effective strategies to improve writing of adolescents in middle and high schools.* New York, NY: Carnegie Corporation.

Hillocks, G., Jr. (1984, November). What works in teaching composition: A meta-analysis of experimental treatment studies. *American Journal of Education, 93*(1), 133–170.

Hillocks, G., Jr. (1986). *Research on written composition: New directions for teaching.* Urbana, IL: ERIC/NCRE.

Hillocks, G., Jr. (1993). Environments for active learning. In L. Odell (Ed.), *Theory and practice in the teaching of writing: Rethinking the discipline* (pp. 244–270). Carbondale, IL: Southern Illinois University Press.

Hillocks, G., Jr. (1995). *Teaching writing as reflective practice.* New York, NY: Teachers College Press.

Hillocks, G., Jr. (1999). *Reflective thinking, reflective teaching.* New York, NY: Teachers College Press.

Hillocks, G., Jr. (2005). The focus on form vs. content in teaching writing. *Research in the Teaching of English, 40*(2), 238–248.

Hillocks, G., Jr. (2010). Teaching argument for critical thinking and writing: An introduction. *English Journal, 99*(6), 24–32.

Hillocks, G., Jr. (2011). *Teaching argument writing, grades 6–12: Supporting claims with relevant evidence and clear reasoning.* Portsmouth, NH: Heinemann.

Hillocks, G., Jr., Kahn, E., & Johannessen, L. (1983). Teaching defining strategies as a mode of inquiry. *Research in the Teaching of English, 17,* 275–284.

Holzman, L. (2009). *Vygotsky at work and play.* New York, NY: Routledge.

Juzwik, M. M., Borsheim-Black, C., Caughlan, S., & Heintz, A. (2013). *Inspiring dialogue: Talking to learn in the English classroom.* New York, NY: Teachers College Press.

Langer, J. A. (2001, Winter). Beating the odds: Teaching middle and high school students to read and write well. *American Education Research Journal, 38*(4), 837–880.

McCann, T. M. (1996). A pioneer simulation for writing and for the study of literature. *English Journal, 85*(3), 62–67.

McCann, T. M. (2014). *Transforming talk into text: Argument writing, inquiry, and discussion.* New York, NY: Teachers College Press.

McCann, T. M., Johannessen, L. R., Kahn, E., & Flanagan, J. (2006). *Talking in class: Using discussion to enhance teaching and learning.* Urbana, IL: National Council of Teachers of English.

Moreau, J. (2004). *Schoolbook nation: Conflicts over American history textbooks from the Civil War to the present.* Ann Arbor, MI: University of Michigan Press.

National Council for Social Studies (NCSS). (2013). *The College, Career, and Civic Life (C3) Framework for social studies state standards: Guidance for enhancing the rigor of K–12 civics, economics, geography, and history.* Silver Spring, MD: Author.

Newmann, F. M., Marks, H. M., & Gamoran, A. (1996, August). Authentic pedagogy and student performance. *American Journal of Education, 104,* 280–312.

Nystrand, M. (1997). *Opening dialogue: Understanding the dynamics of language and learning in the English classroom.* New York, NY: Teachers College Press.

Parker, W. C. (2003). *Teaching democracy: Unity and diversity in public life.* New York, NY: Teachers College Press.

Parker, W. C. (Ed.). (2010). *Social studies today: Research and practice.* New York, NY: Routledge.

Ravitch, D. (2013). Robert D. Shepherd: Beware the social engineer and his abstractions. Available at dianeravitch.net/2013/06/12/robert-d-shepherd-beware-the-social-engineer-and-his-abstractions/

Roop, P., & Roop, C. (1986). *Buttons for General Washington.* Minneapolis, MN: Carolrhoda Books.

Schultz, K. (2009). *Rethinking classroom participation: Listening to silent voices.* New York, NY: Teachers College Press.

Shaffer, D. W., Squire, K. R., Halverson, R., & Gee, J. P. (2005). Video games and the future of learning. *Phi Delta Kappan, 87*(2), 105–111.

Smagorinsky, P. (1991). *Expressions: Multiple intelligences in the English classroom.* Urbana, IL: National Council of Teachers of English.

Smagorinsky, P. (2010, July). EJ Extra: Is it time to abandon the idea of "best practices" in the teaching of English? *English Journal, 98*(6), 15–22.

Smagorinsky, P., Johannessen, L. R., Kahn, E., & McCann, T. M. (2010). *The dynamics of writing instruction: A structured process approach for middle school and high school.* Portsmouth, NH: Heinemann.

Smagorinsky, P., Johannessen, L. R., Kahn, E. A., & McCann, T. M. (2011). *Teaching students to write argument (Dynamics of writing instruction).* Portsmouth, NH: Heinemann.

Smith, M. W., & Wilhelm, J. D. (2006). *Going with the flow: How to engage boys (and girls) in their literacy learning.* Portsmouth, NH: Heinemann.

Smith, M. W., Wilhelm, J. D., & Fredricksen, J. E. (2012). *Oh, yeah?! Putting argument to work both in school and out.* Portsmouth, NH: Heinemann.

Toulmin, S. E. (2000). *The uses of argument.* Cambridge, U.K.: Cambridge University Press. (Original work published 1958)

Troyka, L. Q. (1974). *A study of the effect of simulation-gaming on expository prose competence of college remedial English composition students.* Doctoral dissertation, University of New York. (ERIC Document Reproduction Service No. ED 090 541)

Troyka, L. Q., & Nudelman, J. (1975). *Taking action: Writing, reading, speaking, and listening through simulation-games.* New York, NY: Prentice-Hall.

Tyler, R. W. (1969). *Basic principles of curriculum and instruction.* Chicago, IL: University of Chicago Press.

Vygotsky, L. (1978). *Mind in society: The development of higher cognitive processes.* Boston, MA: Harvard University Press.

Ward, G., Burns, K., & Burns, R. (1990). *The Civil War.* New York, NY: Vintage.

Wiggins, G., & McTighe, J. (2005). *Understanding by design* (2nd ed.). Alexandria, VA: Association for Supervision and Curriculum Development.

Wiggins, G., & McTighe, J. (2013). *Essential questions: Opening doors to student understanding*. Alexandria, VA: Association for Supervision and Curriculum Development.

Willingham, D. T. (2009). *Why don't students like school? A cognitive scientist answers questions about how the mind works and what it means for the classroom*. San Francisco, CA: Jossey-Bass.

Wineburg, S., Martin, D., & Monte-Sano, C. (2013). *Reading like a historian: Teaching literacy in middle and high school history classrooms*. New York, NY: Teachers College Press.

Zimmerman, J. (2002). *Whose America? Culture wars in the public schools*. Cambridge, MA: Harvard University Press.

Index

About the Authors

Thomas M. McCann is a professor of English at Northern Illinois University, where he contributes to the teacher certification program. He taught English in high schools for 25 years, including 7 years working in an alternative high school. He has been a high school English department chair, an assistant principal, and an assistant superintendent. His previous book from Teachers College Press, *Transforming Talk into Text*, draws from a 2-year research project that examines the impact that authentic discussions have on students' academic writing. His coauthored books include *In Case You Teach English* (2002), *Supporting Beginning English Teachers* (2005), *Talking in Class* (2006), *The Dynamics of Writing Instruction* (2010), and *Teaching Matters Most* (2012). He coedited *Reflective Teaching, Reflective Learning* (2005). NCTE's Conference on English Education awarded him the Richard A. Meade Award for research about the concerns of beginning teachers.

Rebecca D'Angelo teaches 5th grade at Edison Elementary School in Elmhurst, Illinois. While she has spent the majority of her teaching career at the 5th-grade level, she has had experience with levels kindergarten through 8th grade. She serves on various school district curriculum development teams, focusing on English language arts content development. She conducts workshops at professional conferences at the local, state, and national levels on the subject of writing and disciplinary literacy. Prior to returning to the field of education, she worked in the mortgage banking and advertising industries.

Nancy Galas is a former elementary school teacher and library media specialist. She continues to work as a teacher leader, focusing her efforts on professional development at the local, state, and national levels. Her love of history and reading combined with her belief that learning is a social activity continue to fuel her passion for teaching. Nancy also supervises student teachers and works to inspire a passion for reading and learning in her grandchildren.

Mary Greska is a school library media specialist at Edison Elementary School in Elmhurst, Illinois. At Edison School, she supports teachers and learners with learning in several disciplines, including social studies and language arts, especially writing. Mary's professional passions include incorporating new ways to help students learn through engaging activities and then, with her colleagues, spreading that word at conferences; igniting and nurturing a love of reading in elementary students; and, oddly, geography. In her former life, she was an attorney for a trust company in Chicago but saw the light and made her career change to education.